Special List No. 26

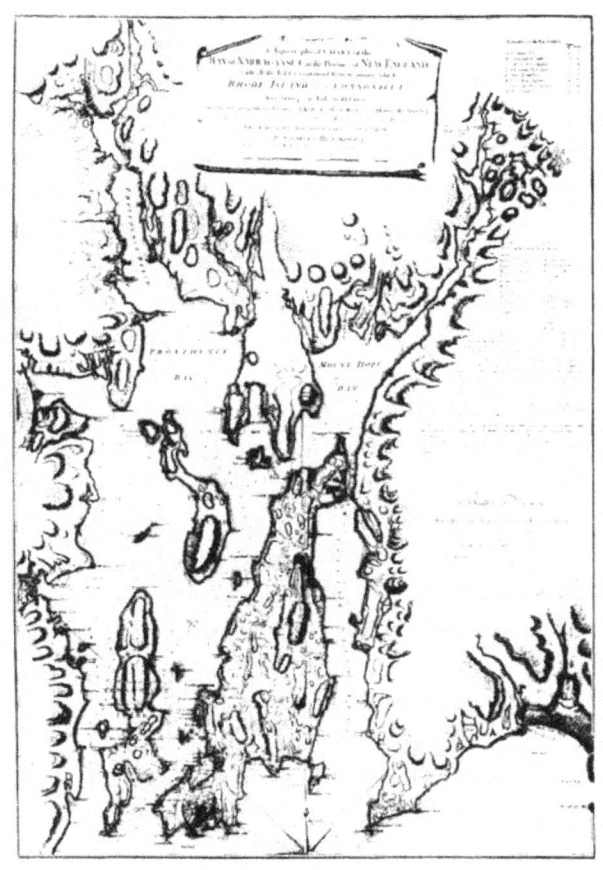

Pre-Federal Maps in the National Archives: An Annotated List

The National Archives
National Archives and Records Service
General Services Administration
Washington: 1971

HERITAGE BOOKS
2013

HERITAGE BOOKS
AN IMPRINT OF HERITAGE BOOKS, INC.

Books, CDs, and more—Worldwide

For our listing of thousands of titles see our website
at
www.HeritageBooks.com

A Facsimile Reprint
Published 2013 by
HERITAGE BOOKS, INC.
Publishing Division
5810 Ruatan Street
Berwyn Heights, Md. 20740

Originally published:
The National Archives
National Archives and Records Service
General Services Administration
Washington: 1971

Richard Nixon
President of the United States

Robert L. Kunzig
Administrator of General Services

James B. Rhoads
Archivist of the United States

Cover Map: Narragansett Bay, 1777. Filed in the Records of the Office of the Chief of Engineers, Record Group 77, in the National Archives Building and described in entry 142 of this special list.

— Publisher's Notice —
In reprints such as this, it is often not possible to remove blemishes from the original. We feel the contents of this book warrant its reissue despite these blemishes and hope you will agree and read it with pleasure.

International Standard Book Numbers
Paperbound: 978-0-7884-9505-2
Clothbound: 978-0-7884-9237-2

Foreword

The General Services Administration, through the National Archives and Records Service, is responsible for administering the permanent noncurrent records of the Federal Government. These archival holdings, now amounting to more than 900,000 cubic feet, date from the days of the First Continental Congress and consist of the basic records of the legislative, judicial, and executive branches of our Government. The Presidential libraries of Herbert Hoover, Franklin D. Roosevelt, Harry S. Truman, Dwight D. Eisenhower, John F. Kennedy, and Lyndon B. Johnson contain the papers of those Presidents and many of their associates in office. While many of the archival holdings document events of great moment in our Nation's history, most of them are preserved because of their continuing practical use in the ordinary processes of government, for the protection of private rights, and for the research use of scholars and students.

To facilitate the use of the records and to describe their nature and content, archivists prepare various kinds of finding aids. The present work is one such publication. We believe that it will prove valuable to anyone who wishes to use the records it describes.

ROBERT L. KUNZIG
Administrator of General Services

Preface

Special lists are published by the National Archives as part of its records description program. The special list describes in detail the contents of certain important records series, that is, units of records of the same form or that deal with the same subject or activity or that are arranged serially. Its form and style are not fixed but vary according to the nature of the records to which it relates. Its distinguishing characteristic is that it goes beyond the general description contained in a record group registration statement, a preliminary inventory, or an inventory, and describes records in terms of individual record items.

In addition to lists and other finding aids that relate to particular record groups, the National Archives publishes some that give an overall picture of materials in its custody. A comprehensive *Guide to the Records in the National Archives* (1948) and a brief guide, *Your Government's Records in the National Archives* (revised 1950), have been issued. A guide devoted to one geographical area—*Guide to Materials on Latin America in the National Archives* (1961)—has been published. Forty-six *Reference Information Papers*, which analyze records in the National Archives on such subjects as transportation, small business, and the Middle East, have so far been issued. Records of the Civil War are described in *Guide to Federal Archives Relating to the Civil War* (1962), *Guide to the Archives of the Government of the Confederate States of America* (1968), and *Civil War Maps in the National Archives* (1964); those of World War I in *Handbook of Federal World War Agencies and Their Records, 1917-1921* (1943); and those of World War II in the two-volume guide, *Federal Records of World War II* (1950-51). Genealogical records are described in *Guide to Genealogical Records in the National Archives* (1964). Among the holdings of the National Archives are large quantities of audiovisual materials received from all sources: Government, private, and commercial. The *Guide to the Ford Film Collection in the National Archives* (1970) describes one of the largest private gift collections. Many bodies of records of high research value have been microfilmed by the National Archives as a form of publication. Positive prints of these microfilm publications, many of which are described in the current *List of National Archives Microfilm Publications,* are available for purchase.

JAMES B. RHOADS
Archivist of the United States

Contents

	Page
Introduction	1
Part I. Atlases	5
1. U.S. Constitution Sesquicentennial Atlas	5
2. George Washington Bicentennial Atlas	6
3. Faden Atlas of the American Revolution	9
Part II. Mapes encompassing two or more Colonies or States	13
Part III. Maps of areas within individual Colonies or States	23
Florida	23
Georgia	24
Louisiana	25
Maine	25
Massachusetts	26
New Hampshire	26
New Jersey	26
New York	27
North Carolina	31
Ohio	31
Pennsylvania	31
Rhode Island	33
South Carolina	33
Vermont	34
Virginia	35
Index	37

Illustrations

A Plan of Boston, 1775 . . . . facing page 5

A Survey of Lake Champlain, 1794 . . . . facing page 13

Sandy Hook, N.J., 1778 . . . . facing page 23

Introduction

A basic function of the National Archives and Records Service (NARS) is to maintain the permanently valuable noncurrent records of the Federal Government. By implication these records should be dated after 1787; but in fact a significant amount of material from the pre-Federal period of American history is also among NARS holdings, including a number of early maps.

Most of the relatively accurate maps and charts of areas in North America at the time of the American Revolution had been compiled by the British, largely in response to the needs of commercial navigation and the requirements of the long series of military campaigns conducted against the French during the 17th and 18th centuries in the struggle for mastery of the continent. Prominent among these documents were the coast charts of *The English Pilot*, a massive work compiled by various individuals and published in more than 30 editions during the period 1671-1784; the charts of *The Atlantic Neptune*, compiled under the direction of Joseph Frederick Wallet des Barres from 1763 to 1774 and published in 1779; Henry Popple's *Map of the British Empire in America*, published in 1733; and the numerous American atlases assembled and published during the late 18th century by Thomas Jefferys and his successor, William Faden, from the best available works by contemporary surveyors and cartographers of all nations.

Significant mapping was also accomplished before and during the Revolution by several native Americans and a number of Englishmen and other Europeans who had settled permanently in the Colonies. Some notable examples are Capt. Cyprian Southack's *The New England Coasting Pilot...*, 1719-33; the *Map of the most Inhabited Part of Virginia containing the whole Province of Maryland...* by Joshua Fry and Peter Jefferson, first published in 1754; Lewis Evans' *Map of the Middle British Colonies in North America*, 1755; John Mitchell's *A Map of the British and French dominions in North America...*, 1755 (which played an important role in the boundary negotiations between the United States and Great Britain following the Revolution); and the extensive military mapping executed during the war by General Washington's engineers under the direction of Thomas Hutchins, Robert Erskine, and Simeon DeWitt.

Copies of many of the maps cited above, either in the original printing or in facsimile form, are among the records in the custody of the Cartographic Archives Division of the National Archives. Much of this material was accumulated in the 19th century by the Army's Corps of Engineers and the Corps of Topographical Engineers (a separate unit in existence from 1838 to 1863) while they were exploring and mapping new territories; planning and surveying roads, canals, and other civil engineering works; and designing and constructing fortifications. These activities necessitated producing and accumulating cartographic aids in the form of maps, sketches, and construction drawings which are now filed with the Headquarters (or Civil Works) File and the Fortifications File in Record Group 77.

Other important early maps in this list were acquired by American diplomatic representatives during negotiations with Great Britain regarding the United States—Canadian boundary following the Revolution. For their own information and for use as evidence in support of U.S. claims, the American commissioners gathered copies of the best available maps covering areas in

North America occupied by Canada and the newly independent United States. Some of these maps have survived and are now among Records of Boundary and Claims Commissions and Arbitrations, Record Group 76.

The 156 items described in this list comprise all the maps in the custody of the Cartographic Archives Division that can be identified as having originated before 1790, as being copies or facsimiles of pre-1790 maps, or as later maps that portray areas or events from the pre-1790 period. The list describes many historically significant items that can, in a real sense, be considered the foundation upon which the vast Federal mapping program was subsequently built. Every new map draws heavily upon the concepts, data, and techniques established by its cartographic forebears, and the training of the early Federal mapmakers was grounded firmly in the French and British traditions of surveying and cartography.

The researcher in the history of American mapping in the colonial and Revolutionary periods will also find particularly rich resources available in the Geography and Map Division of the Library of Congress, the New-York Historical Society, the John Carter Brown Library at Brown University, the American Philosophical Society in Philadelphia, the William L. Clements Library at the University of Michigan in Ann Arbor, and the Newberry Library in Chicago. State and municipal depositories such as the New York Public Library will also prove, in many cases, to be valuable sources for the researcher.

This list is divided into three parts. Part I lists the maps in three special atlases. The U. S. Constitution Sesquicentennial atlas is composed of loose sheets; the Washington and Faden atlases are bound. Part II comprises maps covering the entire United States or two or more States or Colonies, listed in chronological order. Part III comprises maps relating to specific States or Colonies, listed alphabetically by name of State and thereunder chronologically. For convenience in indicating the geographical coverage of some sheets, reference has been made to States of the United States as they now exist.

Dates cited in the chronological sequences of parts II and III are in most cases dates the maps were compiled or published; a few items are listed under the date of the original survey or of the event depicted although the map, or an edition thereof, was published at a later date. Original titles, punctuation, and spelling have been retained, with three exceptions: superscript letters have not been used, nor have archaic letters "f" for "s" and "v" for "u," and some excessively long titles have been shortened. Where several editions or variations of a map are listed consecutively, titles and other data for subsequent maps are the same as for the first map unless differences are noted. Information enclosed in brackets has been supplied by the compilers of this list.

The approximate scale of each item described is indicated if it can be determined from the map; dimensions, stated in inches, are from edge of the sheet to edge, with the vertical dimension first. Compilation and publication data are in most cases provided on the maps themselves and are given as shown on the map. Insets and annotations are noted.

Each map or series of maps is identified as part of either the Reference Collection in the Cartographic Archives Division or one of the following record groups: Records of the Bureau of the Census, Record Group 29; Records of the Bureau of Land Management, Record Group 49; Records of the Bureau of Indian Affairs, Record Group 75; Records of Boundary and Claims

Commissions and Arbitrations, Record Group 76; Records of the Office of the Chief of Engineers, Record Group 77; Records of the Office of the Quartermaster General, Record Group 92; Records of Minor Congressional Commissions, Record Group 148; Records of the United States House of Representatives, Record Group 233; and Records of the Continental and Confederation Congresses and the Constitutional Convention, Record Group 360. Individual file numbers are also indicated for most maps. The Records of the Office of the Chief of Engineers, Record Group 77, include two different types of file numbers: an alpha-numeric designation for items from the Headquarters File, and drawer and sheet numbers for items from the Fortifications File; e.g., Dr. 64, Sht. 5.

With the exception of a few items covered by copyright, photoreproductions of the maps described can be furnished for a fee. Requests for information should be addressed to the Cartographic Archives Division, National Archives (GSA), Washington, DC 20408.

The assistance of Katherine S. Meredith in preliminary cataloging and in preparing the index is gratefully acknowledged.

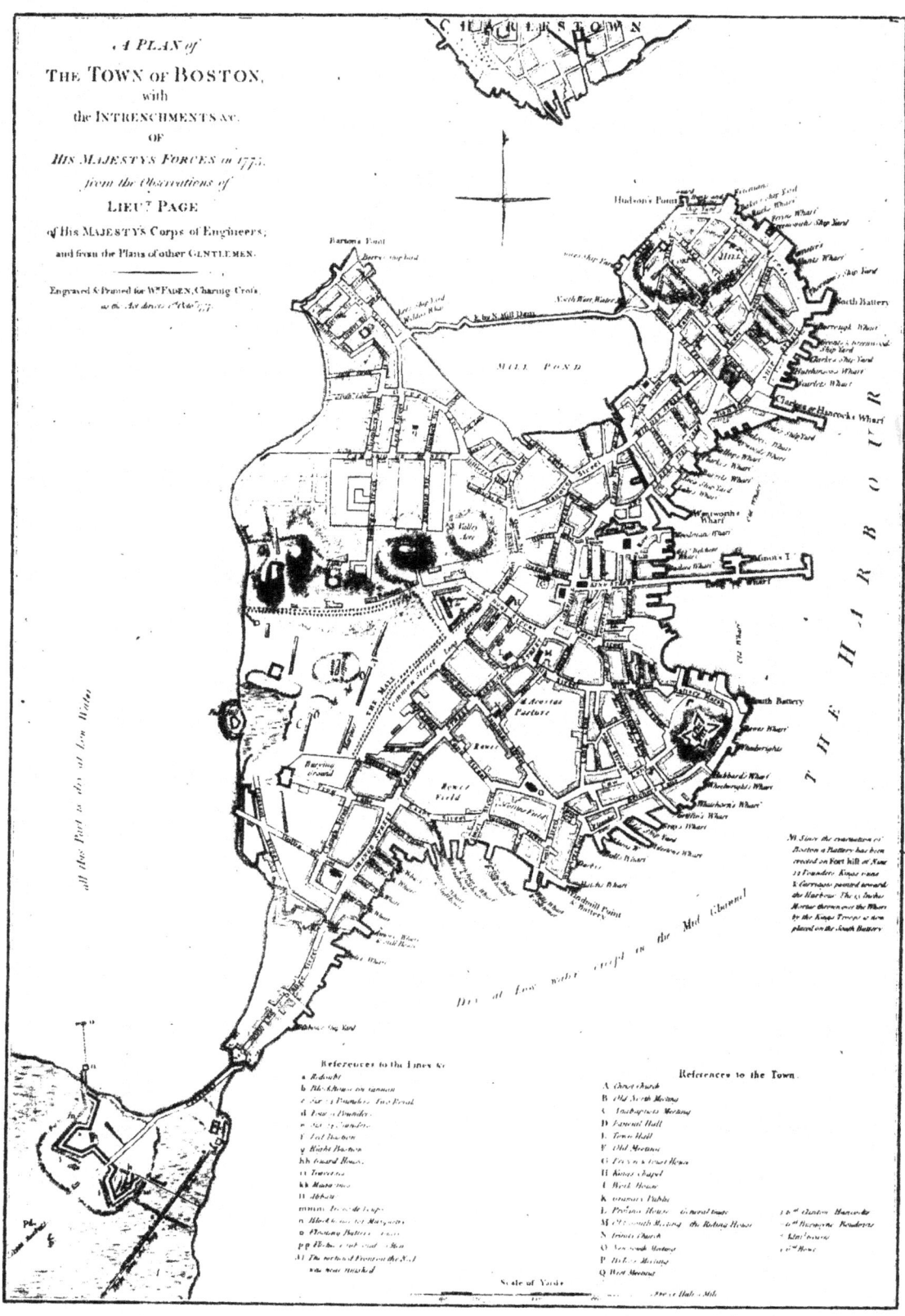

Boston, Mass., 1775. Filed in Records of the Office of the Chief of Engineers, Record Group 77, as part of the Faden atlas, and described in entry 3(2).

Part I. Atlases

1. U.S. Constitution Sesquicentennial Atlas.

During the period 1936-39 the Geological Survey printed a series of facsimiles of early maps of the United States and the Thirteen Original Colonies for distribution in atlas form by the U. S. Constitution Sesquicentennial Commission. These maps were drawn at varying scales. In the facsimile series, most maps were reduced considerably, and each was printed on a uniform 26- by 20-inch sheet. A set of the maps is filed in Records of Minor Congressional Commissions, Record Group 148.

Listed below are the map titles as they appear on the 19 facsimile sheets, followed by shortened titles (appearing in quotations) of the original maps.

1(1). Connecticut at the time of the Ratification of the Constitution, from a 1780 original in the Library of Congress at Washington. "Connecticut, and Parts Adjacent [by Bernard Romans, 1777] at Amsterdam."

1(2). Delaware at the time of the Ratification of the Constitution, from a 1787 original in the Library of Congress at Washington. "This Map of the Peninsula Between Delaware and Chesopeak Bays ... by John Churchman."

1(3). Georgia at the time of the Ratification of the Constitution from an original map in the Library of Congress at Washington. "A General Map of the Southern British Colonies in America ... by B. Romans, 1776." [Two insets.]

1(4). Maryland at the time of the Ratification of the Constitution, from 1780 and 1794 originals in the Library of Congress at Washington. "Map of the State of Maryland ... by Dennis Griffith, June 20, 1794." [One inset.]

1(5). Massachusetts (without the District of Maine) at the time of the Ratification of the Constitution, from original maps in the Library of Congress at Washington. "A Map of the Most Inhabited Part of New England ... 1774." [Two insets.]

1(6). Massachusetts (eastern part; i.e., the District of Maine) at the time of the Ratification of the Constitution, from original maps in the Library of Congress, Washington, including one based upon a Mitchell map owned and used by John Jay, first Chief Justice of the United States. "Extract from a Map of the British & French Dominions in North America by Jno. [John] Mitchell ... 1775." [Two insets.]

1(7). New Hampshire at the time of the Ratification of the Constitution, from a 1784 original in the Library of Congress at Washington. "An Accurate Map of the State and Province of New Hampshire ... by Col. Blanchard and the Rev. Mr. [John] Langdon. [One inset.]

1(8). New Jersey at the time of the Ratification of the Constitution, from an original map in the Library of Congress at Washington. "The Province of New Jersey ... Second edition ... 1778."

1(9). New York at the time of the Ratification of the Constitution, from 1776 and 1787 originals in the Library of Congress at Washington. "A Map of the Province of New York ... 1776."

1(10). North Carolina (eastern part, without Tennessee) at the time of the Ratification of the Constitution, from an original map in the Library of Congress at Washington. "Map of North & South Carolina." [1787.]

1(11). North Carolina (western part; i.e., Tennessee) at the time of the Ratification of the Constitution, from 1788 and 1794 maps in the Library of Congress at Washington. "A Map of the Tennessee Government." [Inset: "A Map of the United States."]

1(12). Pennsylvania at the time of the Ratification of the Constitution, from an original map in the Library of Congress at Washington. "Map of Pennsylvania." [1787.]

1(13). Rhode Island and Providence Plantations at the time of the Ratification of the Constitution, from 1777 and 1795 originals in the Library of Congress at Washington. "Chart of Bay of Narraganset." [1777. Inset: "The State of Rhode Island."]

1(14). South Carolina at the time of the Ratification of the Constitution, from 1780 and 1802 originals in the Library of Congress at Washington. "A Map of South Carolina." [1780.]

1(15). Virginia (eastern part, including West Virginia) at the time of the Ratification of the Constitution, from original 1787 and 1775 maps in the Library of Congress at Washington, one made by Thomas Jefferson, the other by his father [Peter Jefferson]. "A Map ... of Virginia, Maryland, Delaware and Pennsylvania." [1787.] "A Map ... of Virginia." [1775.]

1(16). Virginia (western part; i.e., Kentucky) at the time of the Ratification of the Constitution, from 1784 and 1789 maps in the Library of Congress at Washington. "Map of Kentucke."

1(17). The United States of America showing the boundaries fixed in 1782 five years before the Ratification of the Constitution, from a contemporary copy of Benjamin Franklin's red-line map identified in Spain by the Library of Congress at Washington.

1(18). Inauguration of Gen. George Washington as the first President of the United States of America. Plan of the city of New York; George Washington's Route and Itinerary. John Adams' Route and Itinerary.

1(19). The United States of America at the time of the Ratification of the Constitution, from original maps in the American Geographical Society of New York and the Library of Congress at Washington. "Map of the United States of America." [1783.]

2. George Washington Bicentennial Atlas.

In 1932 the George Washington Bicentennial Commission published an atlas containing 85 maps on 50 plates, "including twenty-eight made by George Washington, seven used and annotated by him, and forty-two new maps concerning his activities in peace and war and his place in history." Dimensions vary. A copy of this atlas is filed in Records of Minor Congressional Commissions, Record Group 148.

Listed below are titles and descriptions of the 85 maps as they appear on the 50 plates.

2(1). General map of George Washington's principal routes of travel, with insert map of his sea voyage to Barbados in 1751-2.

2(2). Mount Vernon. George Washington's own map of all his farms, drawn in 1793.

2(3). Mount Vernon. The River Farm in 1766 (upper); plan of Lawrence Washington's turnip field in 1748 (lower left); sketch of part of the estate near the Mansion House and Little Hunting Creek about 1747 (lower right). All three maps were made by George Washington.

2(4). Mount Vernon. The Dogue Run farm as mapped by George Washington in 1799.

2(5). Mount Vernon. The Union Farm (left); the field and stream near the Potomac River and Little Hunting Creek about 1747 (right). Both maps were made by George Washington.

2(6). Mount Vernon. Roads leading to the Ferry Landing in 1790 (upper); the "Chappel Land" between Accotink Creek and Piney Run (lower left); the roads from Mount Vernon to Pohick Church and to Cameron at some time after 1790 (lower right). All three maps were made by George Washington.

2(7). Mount Vernon. The Mansion House Grounds. The upper middle map is a facsimile of one made by George Washington about 1784. The other three maps were made by Samuel Vaughan in 1781, when he was corresponding with Washington about the landscape gardening of the place.

2(8). Wakefield or Bridges Creek, Westmoreland County, Virginia, where George Washington was born. The upper map is thought to have been made by George Washington in 1747. The lower map is a modern one showing the locations of the birthplace and burial place in relation to Pope's Creek, Bridges Creek, and the Potomac River.

2(9). Washington's Boyhood Home. Part of Rappahannock Farm, or Ferry Farm, or Pine Grove. The words upon the map in George Washington's handwriting are taken from his survey notes of September 13, 1771. The insert map shows the relation of the land mapped by Washington to Fredericksburg, Falmouth, Deep Run, and Little Falls Run [Va.].

2(10). Bath or Warm Springs, now Berkeley Springs, West Virginia, showing lots 58 and 59 upon which George Washington built a house; the indenture under which he bought the land. The map was not drawn by Washington.

2(11). George Washington's sketch map of the country he traversed in 1753-4 between Cumberland, Maryland, and Fort LeBoeuf, near Waterford, Pennsylvania.

2(12). George Washington's own maps of Fort Cumberland, now Cumberland, Maryland, made about 1758 (upper), and of Boston and Cambridge, Massachusetts, made about 1775 (lower).

2(13). Fort Loudoun at Winchester, Virginia, drawn by George Washington about 1756 (upper); his plan for a line of march in a forest country in 1758 (lower).

2(14). Robert Erskine's map of New Jersey in 1777, delineated for the use of George Washington by him in sixteen places.

2(15). Part of James Broom's map of the battlefield of the Brandywine [Pa.], made in 1777 and annotated by George Washington in twelve places.

2(16). The attack upon Fort Mifflin [Pa.] on the Delaware River, October 9, 1777 (upper); the redoubts near Philadelphia in 1778 (lower), both maps annotated by George Washington.

2(17). Stony Point and Verplanck's Point, New York, in 1779, annotated by George Washington (upper); Washington's plan of the order of battle for 1781 (lower).

2(18). The left-hand map was drawn by George Washington from an account sent to him by General Edward Hand on March 31, 1779, and shows an area on the Susquehanna River in southern New York and northern Pennsylvania. The right-hand map is a modern one, showing localities where George Washington did surveying.

2(19). George Washington's survey of the site of Belhaven (Alexandria), Virginia, about 1748 (upper); his plan of the town, believed to have been drawn a year later (lower).

2(20). Two simple land surveys made by George Washington on November 17, 1750 (left), and April 3, 1751 (right).

2(21). Two complex surveys, George Washington's land on Four Mile Run, surveyed in April, 1799 (left); a tract on the Potomac near Pawpaw, West Virginia, surveyed in April, 1751 (right).

2(22). The Potomac River near Harpers Ferry [W. Va.] with George Washington's comments on its navigability, 1754 (upper); a tract at the mouth of the Little Kanawha, West Virginia, 1773 (lower). Washington made the upper map and annotated the lower one.

2(23). George Washington's own map of his lands on the Great Kanawha River, West Virginia, drawn from surveys by William Crawford, Samuel Lewis, and John Floyd, between 1771 and 1774. [Map on two pages.]

2(24). Three tracts of Washington's land on the Ohio River in West Virginia between the mouths of the Great and Little Kanawha Rivers. Map drawn by George Washington in 1787.

2(25). Parts of Maryland, Pennsylvania, and West Virginia, to illustrate plans for water transportation from the Atlantic seaboard to the Mississippi valley. The upper map, attributed to George Washington, is here proved by his own annotation of the lower map to have been drawn by Normand Bruce in 1784.

2(26). New England, showing George Washington's journeys in red.

2(27). New York State, showing in red the places visited by George Washington.

2(28). New Jersey, showing in red the places visited by George Washington.

2(29). Pennsylvania, showing in red the places visited by George Washington and the routes of his journeys to Fort LeBoeuf in 1753, with [Gen. Edward] Braddock in 1755, and with [Gen. John] Forbes in 1758.

2(30). Maryland and Delaware, showing in red the places visited by George Washington.

2(31). West Virginia and Ohio, showing in red the places visited by George Washington and the routes of his Ohio River journey in 1770, and his journey across West Virginia in 1784.

2(32). The region of the lower Potomac, showing in red Mount Vernon and the places visited by George Washington.

2(33). Virginia, showing in red the places visited by George Washington.

2(34). North Carolina, South Carolina, and Georgia, showing in red the places visited by George Washington; the insert map gives the route of his whole southern tour in 1791.

2(35). Washington's campaign with Braddock in 1755.

2(36). Washington's campaign in 1776 from Brooklyn to Morristown, via White Plains, Trenton, and Princeton.

2(37). Washington's campaign in 1777 from Morristown to Valley Forge, via the highlands of the Hudson, the Brandywine, and Germantown [Pa.].

2(38). Washington's campaign in 1778 from Valley Forge to the Hudson via Monmouth Court House [N.J.].

2(39). Washington's campaign in 1781 from the Hudson to Yorktown.

2(40). John Trumbull's map of the siege of Boston, made at Washington's direction and sent by him to Congress (upper); a French map of the battle of Monmouth (lower).

2(41). Sebastian Bauman's map of the siege of Yorktown, dedicated to Washington.

2(42). Cambridge and Boston, Massachusetts, showing localities associated with George Washington.

2(43). New York City, showing localities associated with George Washington.

2(44). Newburgh and New Windsor, New York (upper right), Morristown, New Jersey (upper left), Philadelphia (lower), showing localities associated with George Washington.

2(45). Annapolis, Maryland (upper), and Alexandria, Virginia (lower), showing localities associated with George Washington.

2(46). Washington, D.C., showing localities associated with George Washington; insert map on right shows the Patowmack Company's canal and locks at Great Falls, Virginia, parts of which were constructed during the period when Washington was president of the company.

2(47). Fredericksburg, Virginia (upper), and Williamsburg, Virginia (lower), showing localities associated with George Washington.

2(48). The localities in New York, Pennsylvania, Ohio, Kentucky, West Virginia, the District of Columbia, Maryland, and Virginia where George Washington owned land.

2(49). The world, showing features named for and statues of George Washington outside of continental United States.

2(50). The United States of America, showing features named for George Washington, other than streets, buildings, schools, monuments, etc.

3. Faden Atlas of the American Revolution.

During and shortly after the American Revolution the British publisher, William Faden, produced a series of maps illustrating the principal Revolutionary battles and campaigns. The sheets were assembled and published as an atlas in 1793. In 1845 the New York firm of Bartlett & Welford purchased the Faden sheets and again issued them in atlas form. Among the Records of the Office of the Chief of Engineers, Record Group 77, is a recently bound collection of the original published sheets, together with manuscript tracings based on two of them.

Listed below are the maps as they appear in the atlas, generally including topography, roads, and settlements in battle or campaign areas, and positions and movements of opposing forces.

3(1). A Plan of the Action at Bunker's Hill, on the 17th of June, 1775. Between His Majesty's Troops, Under the Command of Major General [William] Howe, And the American Forces.
1 inch to ca. 150 yards. 22 x 30.

3(2). A Plan of the Town of Boston, with the Intrenchments & c. of His Majesty's Forces in 1775; from the Observations of Lieut. Page of His Majesty's Corps of Engineers; and from the Plans of other Gentlemen.
1 inch to ca. 700 feet. 22 x 15.

3(2a). A manuscript outline tracing of the map listed as 3(2). 20 x 13.

3(3). Plan of the City and Environs of Quebec; with its Siege and Blockade by the Americans, from the 8th of December 1776 to the 13th of May 1776.
1 inch to 600 feet. 22 x 29.

3(4). A Plan of the Attack of Fort Sullivan, near Charles Town [Charleston] Carolina. by a Squadron of His Majesty's Ships, on the 28th of June 1776. with the Disposition of the King's Land Forces, and the Encampments and Entrenchments of the Rebels from the Drawings made on the spot.
1 inch to ca. 2,000 feet. 15 x 22.
Inset: "plan of Fort Sulivan."

3(5). A [north by east] View of the Fort on the Western end of Sulivans Island with the Disposition of His Majesty's Fleet Commanded by Commodore Sir Peter Parker ... during the Attack on the 28th of June 1776 which lasted 9 hours and 40 minutes.
Scale not indicated. 10 x 16.

3(5a). To Commodore Sir Peter Parker ... This View [of Sullivan's Island] is Most humbly dedicated and Presented by Lt. Colonel Thos James ... July 1st 1776.
Scale not indicated. 9 x 23.

3(6). A Topographical Map of the Northn. Part of New York Island, Exhibiting the Plan of Fort Washington, now Fort Knyphausen, With the Rebels Lines to the Southward, which were forced by the Troops under the Command of the Rt. Honble. [Sir Hugh] Earl Percy on the 16th Novr. 1776 ...
1 inch to ca. 1,500 feet. 22 x 15.

3(7). Plan of the Operations of General Washington, against The Kings Troops in New Jersey. from the 26th of December 1776. to the 3d January 1777.
1 inch to ca. 2 miles. 14½ x 22.

3(7a). A [northwest by north] View of Charles Town from on board the Bristol Commodore Sir Peter Parker. ... taken in Five Fathom Hole the day after the Attack upon Fort Sulivan by the Commodore & his Squadron, which Action continued 9 hours & 40 minutes.
Scale not indicated. 10 x 12.

3(8). A Plan of Part of the Provinces of Pensylvania, and East & West New Jersey, showing the Operations of the Royal Army under the Command of their Excellancies Sir Willm Howe & Sir Henry Clinton [in 1777-78].
Scale not indicated. 22 x 29½.

3(9). Battle of Brandywine in which the Rebels were defeated, September the 11th 1777, by the Army under the Command of General Sr. Willm. Howe.

    1 inch to ca. 1,000 feet. 29 x 22.

3(10). British Camp at Trudruffin [Pa.] from the 18th to the 21st of September 1777 with the Attack made by Major General [Charles] Grey against the Rebels near White Horse Tavern [Pa.] on the 20th of September.

    1 inch to ca. ½ mile. 15 x 22.

3(11). The Course of Delaware River from Philadelphia to Chester [Pa.] with the several Forts and Stackadoes raised by the Americans, and the Attacks made by His Majesty's Land and Sea Forces.

    1 inch to ca. ½ mile. 22 x 29½. Inset: "plan of Fort Miffin on Mud Island."

3(12). A Plan of the City and Environs of Philadelphia, with the Works and Encampments of His Majesty's Forces. under the Command of Lieutenant General Sir William Howe K. B.

    1 inch to ca. ¼ mile. 29 x 22.

3(13). Sketch of the Surprise of Germantown. by the American Forces commanded by General Washington. October 4th 1777; by J. Hills.

    1 inch to ca. 1,800 feet. 22 x 29.

3(14). A Map of the Country in which the Army under Lt. General [John] Burgoyne acted in the Campaign of 1777, shewing the Marches of the Army & the Places of the principal Actions.

    1 inch to ca. 10 miles.

3(15). Plan of the Action at Huberton [Vt.] under Brigadier Genl. [Simon] Frazer supported by Major Genl. [Friedrich von] Riedesel, on the 7th of July 1777.

    1 inch to 200 paces. 14½ x 22.

3(16). Position of the Detachment under Lieut. Col. Baum, at Walmscock near Bennington [Vt.] Shewing the Attacks of the Enemy on the 16th August 1777.

    1 inch to 200 paces. 14 x 22.

3(17). Plan of the Encampment and Position of the Army under His Excelly. Lt. General Burgoyne at Swords House on Hudson's River near Stillwater [N.Y.].

    1 inch to 400 yards. 14½ x 22.

3(18). Plan of the Encampment and Position of the Army under His Excelly. General Burgoyne at Braemus Heights on Hudson's River near Still water.

    1 inch to 400 yards. 15½ x 22.

3(19). Plan of the Position which the Army under Lt. Genl. Burgoine took at Saratoga on the 10th of September 1777, and in which it remained till the Convention was signed.

    1 inch to ca. 300 yards. 15 x 22.

3(20). Plan of the Attack of the Forts Clinton & Montgomery [N.Y.], upon Hudsons River which were stormed by His Majestys Forces under the Command of Sir Henry Clinton K. B. on the 6th of Octr. 1777.

    1 inch to ca. 1,800 feet. 29½ x 22.

3(21). A Plan of the Surprise of Stoney Point, by A detachment of the American Army, Commanded by Brigr. Genl. [Anthony] Wayne, on the 15th July 1779.

    Scale not indicated. 22 x 29½.

3(22). Sketch of the Position of the British Forces at Elizabeth Town Point after their Return from Connecticut Farm, in the Province of East Jersey: under the Command of His Excelly. Leiutt. [Gen. Wilhelm von Knyphausen] on the 8th June 1780.

    1 inch to 200 paces. 29 x 22.

3(23). Plan of the Siege of Savannah, with the joint Attack of the French and Americans on the 9th October 1779 In which they were defeated by his Majesty's Forces under the Command of Major Genl. Augustin Prevost, From A survey by an Officer.

    1 inch to ca. 400 feet. 22 x 29.

3(24). The Marches of [Maj. Gen. Charles] Lord Cornwallis in the Southern Provinces, now States of North America; Comprehending the Two Carolinas, with Virginia and Maryland, and the Delaware Counties.

    1 inch to ca. 25 miles. 28½ x 22.

3(25). Plan of the Siege of Charlestown in South Carolina.
   1 inch to ca. 1,800 feet. 15 x 22.

3(26). Battle of Guildford [Courthouse, N.C.], Fought on the 15th of March, 1781. [and] Plan of the Battle Fought near Camden [S.C.] August 16th 1780.
   Scales vary. Two maps on a single sheet. 14½ x 22.

3(27). Sketch of the Battle of Hobkirks Hill [S.C.], near Camden, on the 25th April, 1781.
   Scale not indicated. 22 x 15.

3(28). Sketch of the Skirmish at Petersburg [Va.], between the Royal Army under the Command of Major Genl. Phillips, and the American Army commanded by Major Genl. [von] Stewben; in which the latter were defeated April 25th 1781.
   1 inch to ca. ¼ mile. 15 x 22.

3(29). The Landing at Burrell's [Ferry, Va.] April 17th, 1781.
   1 inch to ca. 1,800 feet. 9½ x 15.

3(29a). Skirmish at Richmond [Va.] Jan: 5th 1781.
   Scale not indicated. 9 x 15.

3(30). Sketch of the Action at Osburns [Va.] April 27th 1781.
   1 inch to ca. ¼ mile. 9½ x 14½.

3(30a). Actions at Spencer's Ordinary [Va.] June 26th 1781.
   Scale not indicated. 10 x 15.

3(31). Suprize of Rebels at Hancocks House.
   Scale not indicated. 9½ x 15.

3(31a). March of the Queens Rangers.
   Scale not indicated. 9½ x 15.

3(32). Affair at Quintin's Bridge [N.J.]. 18th March 1778.
   Scale not indicated. 9½ x 15.

3(32a). Ambuscade of the Indians at Kingsbridge [N.Y.]. August 31st 1778.
   Scale not indicated. 8 x 15.

3(33). A Plan of the Entrance of Chesapeak[e] Bay, with James and York Rivers; wherein are shewn the Respective Positions (in the beginning of October) . . . of the British Army Commanded by Lord Cornwallis, at Gloucester and York [Town] in Virginia; . . . of the American and French Forces under General Washington, . . . and of the French Fleet under Count de Grasse.
   1 inch to 4 miles. 16 x 20.

3(34). Plan of the Siege of York Town in Virginia.
   1 inch to 1,500 feet. 13½ x 21.

3(35). A Plan of York Town and Gloucester, in the Province of Virginia, Shewing the Works constructed for the Defence of those Posts by the British Army . . . together with the Attacks and Operations of the American and French Forces.
   1 inch to ca. 500 feet. 29½ x 21½.

3(36). Battle of Monmouth. Manuscript tracing.
   1 inch to ca. ½ mile. 11½ x 16½.

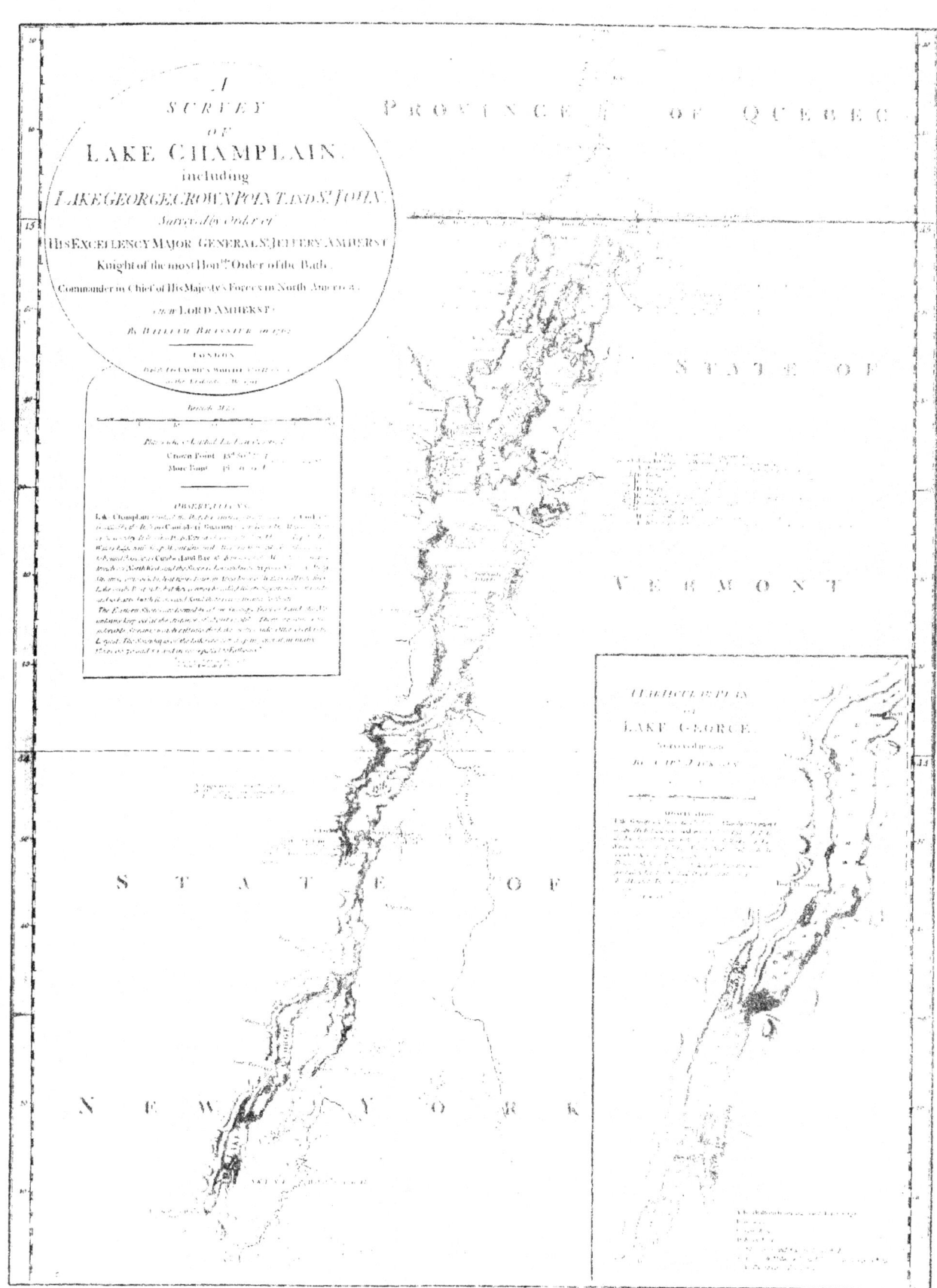

Lake Champlain, 1794. Filed in Records of the Office of the Chief of Engineers, Record Group 77, and described in entry 117.

Part II. Maps Encompassing Two or More Colonies or States

The following maps of areas that overlap Colonial or State boundaries are listed chronologically from ca. 1635 to 1784. In each entry the title is followed by facts of publication, map scale and dimensions, and a brief description, including any insets or annotations. Appearing last is the file location of each map, which indicates whether it is in the Reference Collection of the Cartographic Archives Division or filed in a particular record group. Series numbers and individual file numbers are given where necessary.

ca. 1635

4. Novii Belgii, Quod nunc Novi Jorck vocatur Novae Angliae & Partis Virginae Accuratissima et Novissima Delineatio.

    Published 1876 by the Office of the Chief of Engineers, U. S. Army. 1 inch to ca. 50 miles. 13 x 15½. Shows location of Indian tribes and villages from Virginia to Maine. Annotation: "Facsimile of a map which is supposed to have been printed about A. D. 1635 and is now in the War Department."

    Ref. Coll.

1672

5. Lac Superieur et Autres Lieux ou Sont les Missions des Peres de la Compagnie de Jesus Comprises sous le nom D'Outaouacs.

    1 inch to 30 miles. 21 x 26. Shows location of several missions around Lake Superior and the northern parts of Lakes Michigan and Huron. Annotation: "Facsimile of a Map made by the Jesuit Missionaries in the years 1670 and 1671 and published at Paris 1672. House of Reps. Ex Doc No 69 Sept 1st 30 Congr."

    RG 233: Published maps.

ca. 1713

6. A Map of the West-Indies or the Islands of America in the North Sea; with ye adjacent Countries; explaining what belongs to Spain, England, France, Holland & c. also ye Trade Winds, and ye several tracts made by ye Galeons and Flota from place to place. According to ye Newest and most Exact Observations By Herman Moll Geographer.

    Published ca. 1713 by Thomas and John Bowles, London. 1 inch to 75 miles. 25 x 41. Covers the lands around the Caribbean Sea and the Gulf of Mexico, showing towns, forts, missions, Indian villages, and includes descriptive remarks on topography and economic activities. Insets: maps of Veracruz, Mexico, Porto Bello, Panama, Havana, Cuba, Cartagena, Colombia, St. Augustine, Fla., and a view of Mexico City.

    RG 76: Ser. 30, Moll Atlas, No. 10.

1715

7. A New and Exact Map of the Dominions of the King of Great Britain on ye Continent of North America. Containing Newfoundland, New Scotland, New England, New York, New Jersey, Pensilvania, Maryland, Virginia, and Carolina. According to the Newest and most Exact Observations by Herman Moll Geographer.

    Published 1715 by Thomas and John Bowles, London. 1 inch to 50 miles. 41 x 25. Shows generalized topography, towns, and forts. Insets: scene showing beavers building a dam, with Niagara Falls in the distance; plan of Charleston, S. C.; map of North America and northern South America; and map of southeastern United States.

    RG 76: Ser. 30, Moll Atlas, No. 8.

1720

8. A New Map of the North Parts of America claimed by France under ye Names of Louisiana, Mississippi, Canada and New France with ye Adjoyning Territories of England and Spain.

    Compiled 1720 by Herman Moll. 1 inch to ca. 110 miles. 25 x 31. Shows generalized topography, towns, forts, roads, and Indian tribes. Insets: view of the Indian

fort Sasquesehanok, map of Annapolis Harbor, Md., and map of the mouths of the Mississippi and Mobile Rivers.
Rg 76: Ser. 30, Moll Atlas, No. 9.

1746

9. New England, New York, New Jersey and Pensilvania. By H. Moll Geographer.

A published facsimile bearing the printed notation "Post Route Map. Supposed date A. D. 1746." 1 inch to ca. 40 miles. 15 x 19. Shows post road north from Philadelphia to Portsmouth, Maine. Includes notes on post office locations and frequency of postal service.
Ref. Coll.

1749

10. Carte D'un Voyage Fait Dans La Belle Riviere En La Nouvelle France. MDCCXLIX. Par le Reverend Pere Bonnecamps Jesuitte Mathematicien.

A manuscript tracing of the 1749 original in the archives of the Hydrographic Service in Paris. 1 inch to ca. 15 miles. 37 x 40½. Covers the Ohio and upper St. Lawrence valleys and Lakes Erie and Ontario. Annotation on verso: "Rec'd thro' the Dept. of State March 7 1889 from our Legation at Paris, at the request of Lt. Col [Wm. L.] Merrill to whom a copy hereof has been sent March 16, 1889."
RG 77: P424.

1749

11. A Map of Pensilvania, New-Jersey, New-York, and the Three Delaware Counties.

A published facsimile of the original map by Lewis Evans. 1 inch to ca. 15 miles. 28 x 22½. Shows generalized topography, roads, and settlements. Includes notes on topography, climate, and on the compilation of the map, with a table of distances between major cities.
Ref. Coll.

1752

12. Carte de la Louisiane Par Le Sr. [Jean Baptiste] d'Anville. Dressee en Mai 1732. Publiee en 1752.

Published by G[uillaume] de la Haye, Paris. 1 inch to ca. 15 miles. 22 x 40. Shows towns, forts, and Indian villages. Inset: map of upper Louisiana.
Ref. Coll.

1752

13. North America. Performed under the Patronage of Louis Duke of Orleans, First Prince of the Blood; By the Sieur d'Anville. Greatly Improved by Mr. [S.] Bolton.

Engraved by R. W. Seale and published 1752 by John and Paul Knapton, London. 1 inch to 100 miles. 37 x 34. Inset: map of the Hudson's Bay-Labrador-Greenland area.
Ref. Coll.

1754

14. Fort Du Quesne [Pittsburgh, Pa.] 1754.

Manuscript plan of the fort, probably compiled during the 19th century. Scale cannot be determined. 12½ x 19½. Annotation "No. 3" in upper left corner suggests plan was part of a series.
RG 77: Dr. 145, Sht. 19/1.

1754

15. George Washington's Map, Accompanying His "Journal to the Ohio," 1754.

Published facsimile of the original. 1 inch to ca. 18 miles. 21½ x 17½. Shows forts and settlements in the region around the junction of the Allegheny and Monongahela Rivers. Includes description of the southward advance of the French from their forts on Lake Erie to block English settlement.
Ref. Coll.

1755

16. A general Map of the Middle British Colonies, in America; Viz Virginia, Mariland, Delaware, Pensilvania, New-Jersey, New-York, Connecticut, and Rhode Island: of Aquanishuonigy, the Country of the Confederate Indians; Comprehending Aquanishuonigy proper, their Place of Residence, Ohio and Tiuxsoxruntie their Deer-Hunting Countries, Couxsaxrage and Skaniadarade, their Beaver-Hunting Countries; Of the Lakes Erie, Ontario and Champlain, And of Part of New-France: Wherein is also shewn the antient and present Seats of the Indian Nations.

A facsimile of the original which was compiled and published in 1755 by Lewis Evans. 1 inch to ca. 25 miles. 23 x 31. Shows generalized topography, roads, and settlements. Includes tables of distances between cities. Inset: map of the Illinois Country.
Ref. Coll.

1760
17. A map of Canada and the North Part of Louisiana with the Adjacent Countrys.
Compiled and published 1760 by Thomas Jefferys, London. 1 inch to 175 miles. 13½ x 21½. Covers southern Canada and the northeastern and northcentral regions of the United States, showing generalized topography, towns, forts, and Indian tribes and villages.
RG 76: Ser. 8, No. 48.

ca. 1762
18. A Map of the British and French Dominions in North America with the Roads, Distances, Limits, and Extent of the Settlements, Humbly Inscribed to the Right Honourable The Earl of Halifax, And the other Right Honourable The Lords Commissioners for Trade & Plantations, By their Lordships Most Obliged and very humble Servant Jno. Mitchell.
Engraved by Thomas Kitchin and published by the author; second English edition, issued probably before 1762. (Publication data on this map and its variants cited below are based on Hunter Miller, *Treaties and other International Acts of the United States of America*, vol. 3.) 1 inch to ca. 30 miles. 54 x 77. Shows streams, generalized topography, towns, forts, roads, trails, and Indian tribes and villages. Includes textual information on the astronomical determinations of various geographical locations in North America and on the sources consulted in the compilation of the map. Inset: map of Labrador-Hudson's Bay region. Annotations: faint penciled line between the highlands and a point slightly west of the northwest branch of the Connecticut River; and "X" near the north end of Ourangabena Lake.
RG 76: Ser. 27.

19. Second copy of the above map. Same title and information as described in entry 18. 60 x 82 (on 8 sheets).
RG 76: Ser. 27.

20. Same title and information as described in entry 18 except publication date which was ca. 1774 (third English edition). 54 x 76 (on 8 sheets).
RG 76: Ser. 27.

21. A Map of the British Colonies in North America with the Roads, Distances, Limits, and Extent of the Settlements, Humbly Inscribed to the Right Honourable the Earl of Halifax, and the other Right Honourable The Lords Commissioners for Trade & Plantations, By their Lordships Most Obliged, and very Humble Servant Jno. Mitchell.
Fourth English edition of entry 18, published 1775. 58½ x 85½ (on 8 sheets). Annotations: locations of several forts and missions, and the word "Barrington," at the southern tip of Nova Scotia.
RG 76: Ser. 27.

22. Same title and information as map cited in entry 21. 53 x 77. Annotations: "B. F. Stevens's Facsimile of the Red-Line-Map in the British Museum K118d26. the lines colourings and notes being reproduced on an uncoloured copy of the same issue of the original map. 22 June 1897"; international water boundaries and the Indian treaty line of 1763 have been overprinted.
RG 76: Ser. 27.

23. A Map of the United States in North America with the Roads, Distances, Limits, and Extent of the Settlements, Humbly Inscribed to the Right Honourable The Earl of Halifax, And the other Right Honourable The Lords Commissioners of Trade & Plantations, By their Lordships Most Obliged, and very humble Servant Jno. Mitchell.
Same information as map cited in entry 21. 54½ x 78 inches. Annotations: boundaries between the United States and British and Spanish possessions are overprinted; words "United States" in title have been pasted over original printed words "British Colonies"; and original

pasteboard map jacket is annotated with the name "J. W. Mulligan."
RG 76: Ser. 13.

24. Partial sheet of the above map, identified as having once been used by Benjamin Franklin (see Hunter Miller, op. cit.). Annotations: U.S.-Canada and Quebec-Nova Scotia boundaries are overprinted; reverse side annotated "Dr. Franklin," "Dr. Franklin Eastn. boundy," and "part of United States and odd sheet."
RG 76: Ser. 29.

25. A Map of the British and French Dominions in North America, with the Roads, Distances, Limits, and Extent of the Settlements, Humbly Inscribed to the Right Honourable the Lords Commissioners for Trade & Plantations, By their Lordships Most Obliged and very humble servant Jno. Mitchell.
   Facsimile of the Mitchell map published by the Military Intelligence Division of the Army General Staff; date and edition of original unknown. Same information as map cited in entry 21. 56 x 74 inches. Another facsimile of the Mitchell map is described in entry 1(17).
Ref. Coll.

1763
26. A Map of the British Dominions in North America As Settled by the late Treaty of Peace 1763.
   Author and publisher unidentified. 1 inch to ca. 150 miles. 11 x 15. Shading shows areas ceded by the French. Inset: map of southern Florida.
RG 76: Ser. 8, No. 5.

1763
27. A New Map of the British Dominions in North America; with the Limits of the Governments annexed thereto by the later Treaty of Peace, and settled by Proclamation, October 7th, 1763.
   1 inch to ca. 175 miles. 10½ x 13. Shows towns, forts, and Indian tribes and villages. Annotation: "Engraved for the *History of the War* in the *Annual Register,* and to be placed at the End of the Volume for 1763." Inset: map of southern Florida.
RG 76: Ser. 8, No. 1.

1764
28. A Map of the Country on the Ohio & Muskingum Rivers Shewing the Situation of the Indian Towns with Respect to the Army under the Command of Colonel Bouquet By Thos. Hutchins Asst. Engineer. [and] A Survey of that part of the Indian Country through which Colonel [Henry] Bouquet marched in 1764 By Thomas Hutchins Asst. Engineer. Two maps on a single sheet.
   Published 1848 by Robert Clarke & Co., Cincinnati. First map, 1 inch to ca. 40 miles. Shows forts, trails, and Indian villages in eastern Ohio. Second map, 1 inch to ca. 12 miles. Shows Bouquet's route from Fort Pitt to the Muskingum River, thence downstream. Two maps on sheet, 15 x 11½.
RG 75: No. 1378.

1764
29. A New Map of Georgia, with Part of Carolina, Florida and Louisiana. Drawn from Original Draughts, assisted by the most approved maps and charts. Collected by Eman[ual]: Bowen Geographer to his Majesty.
   Published 1764 by T. Osborne, London. 1 inch to ca. 40 miles. 17 x 23. Shows roads, trails, towns, and Indian villages.
Ref. Coll.

1765
30. Course of the River Mississippi, from the Balise to Fort Chartres; Taken on an Expedition to the Illinois, in the latter end of the year 1765. By Lt. Ross of the 34th Regiment: Improved from the Surveys of that River made by the French.
   Published 1775 by Robert Sayer, London. 1 inch to ca. 15 miles. 46 x 21½. Shows topography, towns, forts, and Indian villages in the lower Mississippi Valley.
RG 76: Ser. 30, Jefferys Atlas, No. 26.

1765
31. Course of the River Mississippi, from the Balise to Fort Chartres; Taken on an Expedition to the Illinois, in the latter end of the year 1765. By Lieut. Ross of the 34th Regiment: Improved from the Surveys of the River made by the French.
   Edition of map described in entry 30,

TWO OR MORE COLONIES OR STATES

published 1794 by Laurie & Whittle, London. Title sheet, covering the mouth of the White River, measures 42 x 34.
Ref. Coll.

1765

32. River Mississippi, from the Balise to Fort Chartres; Taken on an Expedition to the Illinois, in the latter end of the year 1765; By Lieut. Ross of the 34th Regiment: considerably improved from the French and American Surveys.

    Edition of map described in entry 31, published 1800 by Laurie & Whittle, London. 46½ x 16½. Includes inset map of the mouths of the Mississippi River, drawn in 1776 by Alexander Smith.
    Ref. Coll.

ca. 1767

33. Mapa que comprehende la frontera de los Estados de S. M. en la America Septentrional, nuebamente formado Por el Capitan Dn. Nicolas de la Fora, Y el Teniente de America Dn. Jose Urrutia, sobre barias obserbaciones Astronomicas y particulares que hicieron de la Latitud en que se hallan cituados los Presidios, y sobre los mas Celectos Informes y materiales que pudieron recoger.

    Manuscript. 51 x 130 (on 14 sheets). 1 inch to ca. 18 miles. Shows mountain ranges, roads, towns, Indian villages, ranches and estates, mines, and forts in northern Mexico and the southwestern United States.
    RG 77: Ama 38.

1768

34. Map of the Frontiers of the Northern Colonies with the Boundary Line established Between them and the Indians at the Treaty held by S[ir]. Will Johnson at Ft. Stanwix in Novr. 1768.

    Published facsimile of an unidentified map. 1 inch to ca. 15 miles. 23½ x 35½. Shows forts and settlements in the eastern colonies. Inset: Indian boundary line along the lower Ohio Valley, not shown on the larger map.
    Ref. Coll.

1770

35. British Empire in North America with the West India Isles.

    Engraved by Thomas Kitchin and published 1770 by W[illiam]. Richardson, London. 1 inch to ca. 200 miles. 19½ x 15. Shows generalized topography, towns, and Indian tribes and villages in eastern North America, Central America, and the Caribbean Sea.
    RG 76: Ser. 8, No. 3.

1771

36. A New and Accurate Map of North America, Drawn from the Famous Mr. D'Anville with Improvements from the Best English Maps; and Engraved by R. W. Seale; Also the New Divisions according to the late Treaty of Peace, by Peter Bell.

    Published by Carrington Bowles, London. 1 inch to ca. 100 miles. 21 x 26. Shows topography, towns, forts, and Indian tribes and villages in eastern North America.
    RG 76: Ser. 8, No. 8.

1774

37. A Map of the most Inhabited part of New England; containing the Provinces of Massachusetts Bay and New Hampshire, with the Colonies of Connecticut and Rhode Island, Divided into Counties and Townships: The whole by Astronomical Observations.

    Compiled anonymously by John Green [Bradock Mead]. Published 1774 by Thomas Jefferys. 1 inch to 7 miles. 43 x 40. Shows roads, forts, towns, private estates, townships, and counties. Inset: map of Boston Harbor.
    RG 76: Ser. 30, Jefferys Atlas, No. 15.

1775

38. A Map of the most Inhabited part of Virginia containing the whole Province of Maryland with Part of Pensilvania, New Jersey and North Carolina Drawn by Joshua Fry & Peter Jefferson in 1775.

    Published by Sayer and Jefferys, London. 1 inch to ca. 10 miles. 43 x 50 (on 4 sheets). Shows generalized topography, towns, forts, and roads.
    RG 76: Ser. 30, Jefferys, Atlas, No. 22.

39. 1794 edition of the above map. 33½ x 51 (on 2 sheets). Published by Laurie & Whittle, London.
    Ref. Coll.

1775

40. The Coast of West Florida and Louisiana By Thomas Jefferys, Geographer to His Majesty. The Peninsula and Gulf of Florida or Channel of Bahama with the Bahama Islands, By Thos. Jefferys Geographer to His Majesty. [Two titles on single map.]

    Published 1775 by Robert Sayer, London. 1 inch to ca. 22 miles. 21½ x 50 (on 2 sheets). Shows settlements, forts, and offshore soundings along the coast.

RG 76: Ser. 30, Jefferys Atlas, No. 25.

41. The Coast of West Florida and Louisiana, By Thos. Jefferys Geographer to His Majesty.

    Later edition of western half of map cited in entry 40, published 1794 by Laurie & Whittle, London. 14 x 28.

RG 77: Ama 17.

1775

42. A Map of the Country which was the scene of operations of the Northern Army; including the Wilderness through which General [Benedict] Arnold marched to attack Quebec.

    Engraved by Francis Shallus and Published by C. P. Wayne, Philadelphia. 1 inch to ca. 20 miles. 11½ x 9. Shows towns and forts in New Hampshire and parts of New York, Maine, and Quebec.

Ref. Coll.

1775-76

43. Map of the Country which was the scene of Operations of the northern Army Including the Wilderness Through which Genl. Arnold marched to attack Quebec.

    Variant of map cited in entry 42. Engraved by J. Yeager, apparently for use as an illustrative plate in a book. 1 inch to ca. 20 miles. 10 x 8.

Ref. Coll.

1775

44. North America & the West Indies with the opposite Coasts of Europe and Africa. [and] Chart containing the Coasts of California, New Albion, and Russian Discoveries to the North; with The Peninsula of Kamtschatka, in Asia, Opposite Thereto; and Islands, dispersed over the Pacific Ocean, To the North of the Line. [Two titles on single map.]

    Published 1775 by Sayer & Bennett, London. 1 inch to ca. 300 miles. 21 x 46 (on 2 sheets). Shows major cities and location of Indian tribes in the American colonies, and the tracks of numerous voyages of exploring and commercial expeditions in the Pacific Ocean. Includes tables of astronomical observations made at various sites.

RG 76: Ser. 8, No. 7.

1775

45. North America from the French of Mr. D'Anville. Improved with The English Surveys made Since The Peace.

    Published 1775 by Sayer & Bennett, London. 1 inch to ca. 100 miles. 21½ x 29. Shows mountain ranges, towns, forts, and Indian tribes and villages in eastern North America.

RG 76: Ser. 8, No. 11.

1776

46. A chart of Delaware Bay and River, Containing a full and exact description of the Shores, Creeks, Harbours, Soundings, Shoals, Sands and Bearings of the most considerable Land Marks from the Capes to Philadelphia. Taken from the Original Chart Published at Philadelphia by Joshua Fisher.

    Engraved and published 1776 by William Faden, London. 1 inch to ca. 3½ miles. 19 x 28. Shows a few soundings in the bay and settlements along the shore.

RG 77: E18.

47. A General Map of the Northern British Colonies in America, which comprehends The Province of Quebec, The Government of Newfoundland, Nova-Scotia, New-England and New-York. From the Maps Published by The Admiralty and Board of Trade, Regulated by the Astronomic and Trigonometric Observations of Major [Samuel] Holland and corrected from Governor [Thomas] Pownall's Late Map 1776.

    Published by Sayer & Bennett, London. 1 inch to ca. 60 miles. 20 x 26½. Shows generalized topography, towns, and roads.

RG 76: Ser. 8, No. 14.

1776

48. A Map of the Middle British Colonies in North America. First published by Mr. Lewis Evans, of

Philadelphia, in 1775; and since Corrected and improved, as also extended, with the addition of New England, and bordering Parts of Canada; from Actual Surveys now lying at the Board of Trade. By T. Pownall M. P. with a Topographical Description of such parts of North America as are contained in this map.

    Engraved by J[ames]. Turner and published by J. Almon, London. 1 inch to ca. 38 miles. 20½ x 33. Shows generalized topography, roads, and settlements. Table lists names of counties and townships in several New England colonies. Inset: map of the Ohio Country.

RG 76: Ser. 8, No. 53.

1776

49. The Provinces of New York, and New Jersey; with part of Pensilvania, and the Province of Quebec. Drawn by Major Holland, Surveyor General of the Northern District of America. Corrected and Improved from the Original Materials by Govern. Pownall, Member of Parliament, 1776.

    Published by Sayer & Bennett, London. 1 inch to ca. 10 miles. 55 x 21½ (on 2 sheets). Shows topography, roads, forts, towns, and private estates. Insets: chart of the Hudson River mouth, plan of Amboy, N.J., and plan of New York City.

RG 76: Ser. 8, No. 55.

1777

50. A Map of the Provinces of New-York and New-Jersey, with a part of Pennsylvania and the Province of Quebec. from the Topographical Observations of C[laude]. J[oseph]. Sauthier.

    Published facsimile; original was engraved and published by Matthew Albert Lotter, Augsburg, Germany. 1 inch to ca. 12 miles. 43 x 31. Shows settlements, counties, and a few large private estates.

Ref. Coll.

1777

51. A New and Correct Map of North America, with the West India Islands, Divided According to the last Treaty of Peace, Concluded At Paris. 10th Feby. 1763. wherein are particularly Distinguished, The Several Provinces and Colonies which Compose The British Empire, Laid down according to the Latest Surveys, and Corrected from The Original Materials, of Govern. Pownall, Membr. of Parliament 1777.

    Published by Sayer & Bennett, London. 1 inch to ca. 80 miles. 40 x 46 (on 2 sheets). Shows towns, forts, roads, and Indian tribes and villages. Inset: map of Gulf of California.

RG 76: Ser. 8, No. 15a.

52. Copy of upper half of map cited in entry 51, covering only the area from Florida northward. 20½ x 46½ (on 2 sheets).

RG 76: Ser. 8, No. 15b.

1778

53. A New Map of North America From the Latest Discoveries 1778.

    Engraved for Jonathan Carver's *Travels through the interior parts of North America* (London, 1780). 1 inch to ca. 280 miles. 13½ x 15. Shows towns and Indian tribes and villages.

RG 76: Ser. 8, No. 18.

1778

54. A New Map of the Western Parts of Virginia, Pennsylvania, Maryland and North Carolina; Comprehending the River Ohio, and all the Rivers, which fall into it; Part of the River Mississippi, the Whole of the Illinois River, Lake Erie; Part of the Lakes Huron, Michigan &c. And all the Country bordering on these Lakes and Rivers.

    Compiled and published by Thomas Hutchins, 1778. 1 inch to ca. 20 miles. 37 x 44 (on 4 sheets). Shows topography, roads, forts, settlements, and includes many descriptive notes on topography, quality of land, and wildlife.

RG 77: U.S. 6.

1779

55. Carta de las Costas Reconocidas la Norueste de la California.

    Undated manuscript; compiler not identified. 1 inch to ca. 90 miles. 23 x 18. Covers coastal area from San Francisco Bay northward to Prince William Sound, Alaska, showing landfalls by Spanish explorers during the period 1774-79.

RG 77: Ama 135.

1780

56. A Map of South Carolina And a Part of Georgia containing the Whole Sea-Coast; all the Islands, Inlets, Rivers, Creeks, Parishes, Townships, Boroughs, Roads, and Bridges: As Also, Several Plantations, with their proper Boundary-Lines, their Names, and the Names of their Proprietors. Composed from Surveys Taken by the Hon. William Bull Esq. Lieutenant Governor, Captain [John] Gascoign[e], Hugh Bryan, Esq.; and William De Brahm Esqr. Surveyor General of the Southn. District of North America, Republished with considerable Additions, from the Surveys made & collected by John Stuart Esqr. His Majesty's Superintendant of Indian Affairs.

 Published 1780 by William Faden, London. 1 inch to 5 miles. 55 x 49 (on 2 sheets). Shows parishes, private estates, settlements, and roads. Table lists names of principal proprietors and location of their estates.

RG 77: U.S. 8.

1783

57. An Accurate Map of the United States of America, with Part of the Surrounding Provinces agreeable to the treaty of Peace of 1783.

 Compiled and published by John Cary, London. 1 inch to ca. 65 miles. 24½ x 27½. Shows generalized topography, towns, forts, and Indian villages and tribes. Includes text of articles I-III of the treaty.

RG 76: Ser. 8, No. 22.

1783

58. A new map of the United States of North America with the British Dominions on that Continent &c. By Samuel Dunn, Mathematician; Improved from the Surveys of Capt. Carver.

 Published 1783 by Sayer & Bennett, London. 1 inch to ca. 225 miles. 21½ x 14. Shows towns, forts, and Indian tribes. Table lists the States and the remaining British colonies in North America.

RG 76: Ser. 8, No. 24.

1783

59. A new map of North America with the West India Islands. Divided according the Preliminary Articles of Peace, Signed at Versailles, 20 Jan. 1783. Wherein are particularly Distinguished the United States and the Several Provinces, Governments, &ca. which Compose the British Dominions, Laid down according to the Latest Surveys, and Corrected from the Original Materials, of Govern. Pownall, Membr. of Parliamt. 1783.

 1 inch to ca. 80 miles. 21½ x 47 (on 2 sheets). Shows towns, forts, roads, and Indian tribes and villages. Inset: map of Baffin Bay-Hudson's Bay area.

RG 76: Ser. 8, No. 29.

1783

60. The United States of America with the British Possessions of Canada, Nova Scotia, & of Newfoundland, Divided with the French; and the Spanish Territories of Louisiana and Florida according to Preliminary Articles of Peace Signed at Versailles the 20th of Jany. 1783.

 Published 1783 by Sayer & Bennett, London. 1 inch to ca. 100 miles. 21 x 28½. Shows generalized topography, towns, forts, and Indian tribes and villages. Includes text of article III of the treaty.

RG 76: Ser. 30, Jefferys Atlas, No. 19.

1783

61. A New and Correct Map of North America in which the Places of the Principal Engagements during the present War, are accurately Inserted. And the Boundaries as Settled by Treaty in 1783.

 Engraved by John Lodge and published 1783 by John Bew, London. 1 inch to ca. 200 miles. 11½ x 15.

RG 76: Ser. 8, No. 20.

1783

62. The United States of North America with the British & Spanish Territories according to the Treaty, Engraved by Wm. Faden, 1783.

 1 inch to ca. 100 miles. 22 x 30. Shows generalized topography, towns, and Indian tribes and villages.

RG 76: Ser. 8, No. 23.

1783

63. The United States of America laid down From

the best Authorities, Agreeable to the Peace of 1783.

> Published 1783 by John Wallis, London. 1 inch to ca. 100 miles. 20 x 25. Shows generalized topography, towns, Indian tribes, and the Nova Scotia fishing banks. Annotation: "Rec'd from Department of State Washington May 25, 1848."

RG 76: Ser. 8, No. 21.

1783

64. The United States of America, according to the Treaty of Peace of 1784 [1783].

> Compiled and engraved by Russell [first name unknown]. Undated. 1 inch to ca. 200 miles. 8½ x 10.

Ref. Coll.

1784

65. Carte Des Etats-Unis D'Amerique, et du Cours du Mississippi; redigee d'apres differentes Cartes et Relations Anglaises, et les operations de la derniere Guerre avec Les Nouvelles Limites Generales fixees par les articles preliminaires de paix . . . par le Sr. Brion de la Tour.

> Published 1874 by Esnauts & Rapilly, Paris. 1 inch to ca. 70 miles. 21½ x 28. Shows generalized topography, towns, forts, and Indian tribes. Includes table listing population of the individual States. Annotations: Sketched outlines of the new States proposed by Thomas Jefferson for establishment in the Mississippi Valley and the note "Rec'd from Librarian of Congress—7 Jany 1829."

RG 76: Ser. 8, No. 28.

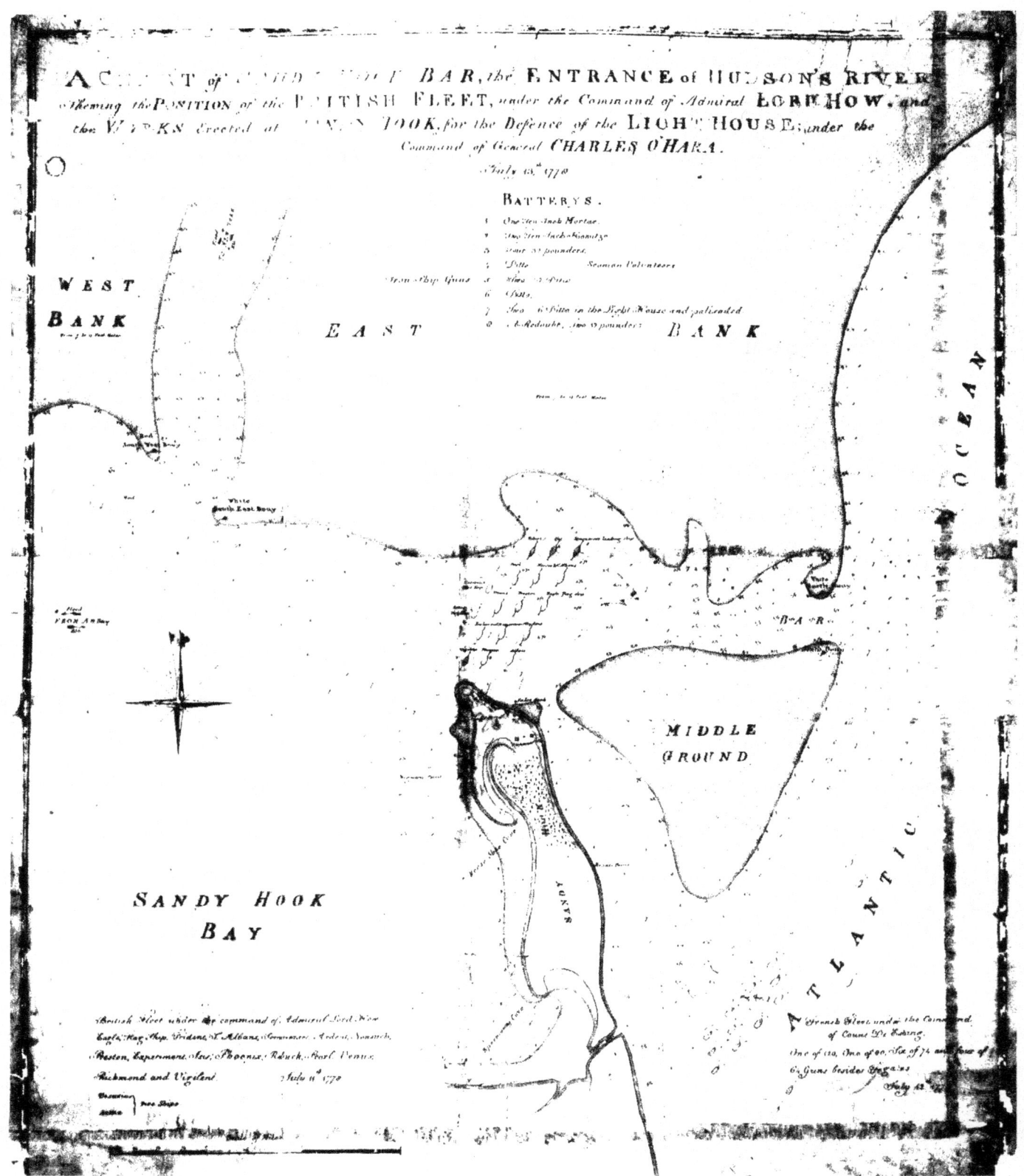

Sandy Hook, N.J., 1778. Filed in Records of the Office of the Chief of Engineers, Record Group 77, and described in entry 106.

Part III. Maps of Areas within Individual Colonies or States

The maps of individual Colonies or States or areas within them are arranged alphabetically by State and thereunder chronologically. In each entry the title is followed by facts of publication, map scale and dimensions, and a brief description, including any insets or annotations. Appearing last is the file location of each map which indicates whether it is in the Reference Collection of the Cartographic Archives Division or filed with a particular record group. Series numbers and individual file numbers are given where necessary.

Florida

1588

66. S Augustini pars est terrae Florida sub latitudinae 30 gradora vero maritima humilior est, lancinata et insulosa.

    Photocopy apparently made from glass-plate negative. Author and publisher unidentified. Scale not indicated. 17 x 22.
    RG 77: Dr. 72, Sht. 28/2.

1605

67. La Citte Sainct Augustin toute Bastie de Maisons . . .

    Photocopy apparently made from glass-plate negative. Author and publisher unidentified. Scale not indicated. 9 x 12. Map is reduced variant of map described in entry 58. File includes blueprint copy.
    RG 77: Dr. 72, Sht. 28/6.

1701

68. A Plan of Pensacola Harbour from 1st Entrance to the Town 1701.

    Manuscript; probably a copy of the original. Compiler unidentified. Scale not indicated. 21 x 30. Shows roads, forts, settlements, and offshor soundings. Inset: plan of Fort Charlotte, southwest of Pensacola.
    RG 77: L5.

1762

69. Plan of the Town and Harbour of St. Augustin.

    Photocopy apparently made from glass-plate negative. Compiler and publisher unidentified. 1 inch to 3/4 mile. 10½ x 13. File includes blueprint copy.
    RG 77: Dr. 72, Sht. 28/4.

1763

70. Piano della Citta e Porto di Sant' Agostino.

    Photocopy apparently made from glass-plate negative. Original was drawn by Giuseppe Pazzi. 1 inch to 3/4 mile. 9½ x 12. Map is an Italian version of map described in entry 61. File includes blueprint copy.
    RG 77: Dr. 72, Sht. 28/5.

1764

71. Plan du Port de St. Augustin dans la Floride.

    Photocopy apparently made from glass-plate negative. Author and publisher unidentified. 1 inch to ca. 2 miles. 9½ x 7½. File includes blueprint copy.
    RG 77: Dr. 72, Sht. 28/10.

1775

72. Hutchins' Plan of the Escambia River.

    Manuscript copy of the original compiled in 1775. 1 inch to ca. 1 mile. 28 x 18. Includes descriptive remarks about physical and cultural features along the river. Annotation: "E33 Escambia River from Hutchins Wilson J. Purcell."
    RG 77: L6/1.

1775

73. A Plan of Amelia Harbour and Barr in East Florida Survey's in Jany. 1775. By Jacob Blainey, Master of his Majesty's Schooner St. John.

    1 inch to ca. ½ mile. 25 x 18½. Shows soundings in the harbor and includes descriptive notes on the bar, the tides, and the winds. Key identifies various features around the harbor. Annotations: "Copied by H. G. Wright, Lt. of Engs., March

1842" and "Copy Sent-informally-to Hon. D. L. Yules Augt. 22, 1879."
RG 77: Dr. 71/1.

1777
74. A Plan of St. Augustine Town and its Environs in East Florida from an Actual Survey made in 1777 by J[oseph]. Purcell Surveyor.
Manuscript. 1 inch to ca. 600 feet. 18 x 27. Includes key to principal streets and buildings.
RG 77: L53/1.

1777
75. Plan of the Town of St. Augustine the Capital of East Florida.
Photocopy apparently made from glass-plate negative; original engraved by Thomas Jefferys and published by William Faden, London. 1 inch to ca. 300 feet. 10½ x 13½. Shows detailed street plan of the town. File includes blueprint copy.
RG 77: Dr. 72, Sht. 28/3.

1778
76. A Map of the Road from Pensacola in W. Florida to St. Augustine in East Florida From a Survey made by Order of the late Hon. Col. John Stuart Esq. His Majesty's Superintend't of Indian Affairs Southern District in 1778 by Joseph Purcell.
Blueline facsimile of the original. 1 inch to ca. 4 miles. 32 x 100 (on 2 sheets). Shows the main road, lesser routes, streams, and Indian villages in northern Florida. Includes a table showing mileages between various points by different routes.
Ref. Coll.

1780
77. A Plan of Cowpen Creek on the East side of Perdido Bay and From its landing Place to Pensacola From a survey performed by Order of Major General Campbell in June 1780 By Joseph Purcell.
Manuscript. 1 inch to ca. 1,500 feet. 21 x 30. Explanatory notes indicate the route of Purcell's survey and a route he suggests as suitable for "a good Carriage Road."
RG 77: L1.

1783
78. A Plan of St. Augustine in East Florida From a Survey in 1783 by Joseph Purcell.
Manuscript tracing "Made in Office of the Chief of Engineers August 1916 from original loaned by Mr. W. W. Dewhurst, St. Augustine, Fla." Scale not indicated. 19 x 28½. Includes key to principal streets and buildings.
RG 77: L53/2.

79. Blue print of map described in entry 78. 19½ x 28.
RG 77: Dr. 72, Sht. 49/13.

1783
80. Plan of the Town and Harbour of St. Augustine, in East Florida.
Photocopy apparently made from glass-plate negative; original engraved by John Lodge and published by John Bew, London. 1 inch to ca. 1 mile. 8½ x 11. Map is a variant of map described in entry 61.
RG 77: Dr. 72, Sht. 28/9.

1785
81. Plano del Castillo de San Marcos en San Agustin de la Florida Oriental.
Manuscript copy drawn in 1884 of the 1785 original from the files of the military engineer headquarters in Madrid. 1 inch to ca. 30 feet. 39 x 25½. Key identifies various parts of the fort. Includes side views of three sections of the fort. Annotation: "Copy sent to Capt. W. T. Russell with letter of Jan. 21, 1885."

1785
82. Plano del Castillo de Sn Marcos cituado a 29 [degrees] y 40 minutos de latitd. en la Florida del Este.
Probably a second manuscript copy of the map cited in entry 81, differing chiefly in title.
RG 77: Dr. 72, Sht. 27.

Georgia

[Undated]
83. A Map of Savannah River beginning at Stone-Bluff, or Nexttobethell, which continueth to the Sea; also, the Four Sounds Savanah, Hossa-

baw, and St. Katharines with their Islands likewise Newport, or Serpent River, from its mouth to Benjehova bluff Surveyed by William Noble of Brahm late Captain Ingenier under his Imperial Majesty Charles the VII.

    Undated manuscript tracing of the original. 1 inch to ca. 2 miles. 28 x 57. Shows towns and roads; coloring distinguishes varying terrain and vegetation types.

RG 77: Z424.

1762

84. Copy of a Survey of Cockspur Island [Ga.] and the Plan of the Fort, at A, as originally made and designed by J. W. G. [Wm] De Brahm. Col. of Engrs. in June 1762.

    Manuscript copy of the original. 1 inch to ½ mile; fort plan drawn at 1 inch to 20 feet. 15½ x 18. Annotation: "This copy was taken from lithographic documents in the possession of Dr. Stevens the Historian of the State of Georgia, who politely granted the favor. At the time this survey was made, the South Channel was the principal channel and used exclusively by large vessels. Fort Pulaski 26th July 1842. J. K. F. Mansfield Capt Corps Engineers."

RG 77: Dr. 70, Sht. 24.

1779

85. Plan of the Siege of Savannah, with the joint Attack of the French and Americans on the 9th October 1779 In which they were defeated by his Majesty's Forces under the Command of Major Genl. Augustin Prevost, From a Survey by an officer.

    Published 1784 by William Faden, London. 1 inch to ca. 400 feet. 16½ x 23. Shows positions of the opposing forces. Annotations: the name "Wilson" and "Rec'd from Maj. Genl. [Alexander] Macomb, Dec. 5th 1839."

RG 77: Dr. 68, Sht. 1.

1780

86. Sketch of the Northern Frontiers of Georgia, extending from the Mouth of the River Savannah to the Town of Augusta, By Archibald Campbell Lieut. Col. 71st Regt.

    Engraved and published 1780 by William Faden, London. 1 inch to ca. 100 miles. 33½ x 25. Shows cultivated areas, roads, and settlements along the lower Savannah River below Ebenezer. Insets show the river above Ebenezer to Augusta.

Ref. Coll.

See also entries 1(3), 2(34), 3(23), and 56.

Louisiana

1744

87. Plan de la Nouvelle Orleans sur le Manuscrits du Depot des Cartes de la Marine. Par N. B. Ingr. de la M. 1744.

    Compiled by Nicolas Bellin; published 1827 in the *Histoire Generale de la Nouvelle France* by P. de Charlevoix. 1 inch to ca. 120 feet. 12 x 14. Key identifies principal buildings in the city.

RG 92: Map 107, Sht. 12.

1778

88. Plan du Lac Ponchartrin dans la Province de la Louisiane, Par la latitude de 30 detrés 36. m. nort. copié apres celui Levé par Jph. Briones Capne. et Pilote de la Goelette au Roy L'industries, par ordre de Don Bernard de Galvez Gouverneur de cette Province L'anée 1778.

    Manuscript. 1 inch to ca. 2½ miles. 17½ x 21½. Shows soundings in the lake.

RG 77: M2

1804

89. Plan of the Mouths and Passes of Mississippi River, from the Mexican Gulf to the upper Confluence of S. W. Pass, drawn in Jany. 1778, and copied at New Orleans in March 1804.

    Manuscript. 1 inch to ca. 1 mile. 28 x 20½.

RG 77: M3/1.

Maine

1705

90. Casco Bay Fort in the Province of Main in America Latitude 44—00.

    Sepia print of original compiled by J. Redknap. 1 inch to ca. 15 feet. 23 x 18. Key identifies individual structures within the fort. Annotation: "Traced March 2, 1904, from copy on file in Collection of Hon. James P. Baxter by C. C. Manning."

RG 77: Dr. 10, Sht. 111/1.

1705
91. Fort at New Casco, Built by Col. Redknap in 1705.
> Sepia print of the original. An oblique view of the fort drawn at an undetermined scale. 8 x 8. Annotation: "Note—The ground plan of this fort was found in the office of the Public Records, London, by James P. Baxter, in 1886."
> RG 77: Dr. 10, Sht. 111/2.

1775
92. Falmouth Neck, as it was when Destroyed by Mowatt, October 18th 1775.
> Sepia print of the original. 1 inch to ca. 250 feet. 17 x 25. Shows area destroyed by the British bombardment.
> RG 77: Dr. 10, Sht. 111/3.

1776
93. Chart of Penobscot Bay and part of Penobscot River State of Maine.
> Published 1776 by J. F. W. Des Barres, London. 1 inch to ca. 2 miles. 45 x 32. Shows topography, streams, and settlements along the coast and on the offshore islands.
> RG 77: A1.
> *See also* entry 1(6).

Massachusetts

1775
94. Boston its Environs and Harbour, with the Rebels Works Raised Against That Town in 1775, from the Observations of Lieut. Page of His Majesty's Corps of Engineers, and from the Plans of Capt. [John] Montresor.
> Engraved and published 1778 by William Faden, London. 1 inch to ca. 2,000 feet. 18 x 34. Shows topography, towns, roads, and fortifications around Boston Bay. Annotation: "Rec'd from Gen Macomb Dec. 5th 1839" and "Engineer Department Washington."
> RG 77: Dr. 19, Sht. 5.

1776
95. A Chart of the Harbour of Boston, With Soundings, Sailing-Marks, &c. Taken From Holland's Surveys Carefully Revised and Corrected, by Osgood Carleton Esqr. Teacher of Mathematics Boston.
> Published by J. F. W. Des Barres, London, and W[illiam]. Norman, Boston. 1 inch to ca. 2,000 feet. 29½ x 41½. Shows city of Boston, soundings in the harbor, and topography of the lands around the harbor.
> RG 77: B1/1.

1776
96. No. 9. Des Barres Map of Boston Harboure Ms.
> Published 1776 by J. F. W. Des Barres, London. 1 inch to ca. 400 feet. 32 x 42½. Shows roads and settlements around Boston Bay.
> RG 77: B1/2.
> *See also* entries 1(5), 2(12, 26, 40, 42), and 3(1, 2, 2a).

New Hampshire

1784
97. A Topographical Map of the Province of New Hampshire, Surveyed agreeably to the Orders and Instructions of the Right Honourable the Lords Commissioners for Trade and Plantationa; unto Samuel Holland Esqr. His Majesty's Surveyor General of Lands for the Northern District of North America By ... Mr. Thomas Wright, Mr. George Sproule, Mr. James Grant, Mr. Thomas Wheeler & Mr. Charles Blaskowitz.
> Published 1784 by William Faden, London. 1 inch to 4 miles. 25 x 35 (on 2 sheets). Shows roads, townships, and settlements.
> Ref. Coll.

98. Second copy of map cited in entry 97 differing slightly in size. 46 x 31 (on 2 sheets).
RG 76: Ser. 8, No. 57.
See also entries 1(7) and 2(26).

New Jersey

1765
99. William Lawrence Map of the Highlands.
> Blueprint of the 1765 original. Scale not indicated. 18 x 27. Shows chain traverses and distances from a survey of the Atlantic Highlands on the New Jersey side of Lower New York Bay. Annotation: "Enclosure 'B' to letter of Dec. 1, 1890."
> RG 77: Dr. 44, Sht. 124/3.

INDIVIDUAL COLONIES OR STATES

1776
100. Sketch of Trenton as it was Decr. 26th 1776.
Photocopy of the original published by H. S. Tanner apparently as an illustrative plate in a book. 1 inch to ca. 3,000 feet. 8 x 13. Shows roads and troop positions and movements.
Ref. Coll.

1777
101. Part of New Jersey, embracing Trenton & Princeton; to exhibit the operations of the American & British Armies, Jany. 1st. 2nd. & 3rd. 1777 with Genl. Washington's previous movements against the Hessians, under Col Rahl, at Trenton. Decr. 25th & 26th. 1776.
Photoreproduction of the original from James Wilkinson, *Diagrams and plans illustrative of the principal battles and military affairs treated of in "Memories of my own times"* (Philadelphia: 1816). 1 inch to 1 mile. 15 x 15. Shows positions and movements of the opposing forces.
Ref. Coll.

1777
102. Military Movements in New Jersey
Photocopy of map from an unidentified book. Scale not indicated. 18 x 12. Shows towns, roads, and troop positions and movements.
Ref. Coll.

1777
103. Battles of Trenton and Princeton.
Photocopy of map from an unidentified book. 1 inch to ca. 1½ miles. 16½ x 10½. Shows topography, roads, and troop positions and movements at the two battlefields. Key locates specific units.
Ref. Coll.

1777
104. Affair of Princeton, January 3rd 1777.
Photocopy of the original from Wilkinson, cited in entry 93. 1 inch to ca. 2 miles. 12½ x 9½. Shows topography, roads, and positions of the opposing forces.
Ref. Coll.

1778
105. The Province of New Jersey Divided into East and West, commonly called the Jerseys.
Engraved and published 1778 by William Faden, London. 1 inch to ca. 7 miles. 32½ x 26. Shows topography, counties, towns, and roads.
Ref. Coll.

1778
106. A Chart of Sandy Hook Bar, the Entrance of Hudson's River; Shewing the Position of the British Fleet, under the Command of Admiral Lord [Richard] How[e]. and the Works Erected at Sandy Hook, for the Defence of the Light House; under the Command of General Charles O'Hara. July 13th, 1778.
Manuscript. 1 inch to ca. 1,800 feet. 39 x 33½. Shows offshore soundings and locations of ships and shore batteries.
RG 77: R8.

107. Blueline facsimile of the map described in entry 106 annotated "Copy of Original Mss. Chart in Archives of U. S. Engineers. Washington, D. C. Reduced Photographic Facsimile made in Office of U. S. Coast & Geodetic Survey, Jan. 1885." 1 inch to ca. 4,000 feet. 16½ x 14½.
Ref. Coll.

1784
108. A Chart of the Bar of Sandy Hook the Entrance of Hudsons River in the Province of New Jersey; Survey'd in 1782, By Lieut. Hills, of the 23d Regt. and private Draftsman To His Excellency the Commander in Chief.
Published 1784 by William Faden, London. Scale not indicated. 28 x 24. Shows offshore soundings and location of Sandy Hook lighthouse.
RG 77: R7.
See also entries 1(8), 2(14, 28, 36-40, 44), and 3(7, 8, 22, 31, 32, 36).

New York

1600-1800
109. Fort, Battles, Batteries on the Niagara Frontier.
Copyright 1919 by Peter A. Porter; apparently an illustrative plate from a book. 1 inch to 2 miles. 18 x 9½. Shows sites of forts and battles along the Niagara River, chiefly from the French and Indian wars and the Revolution.
Ref. Coll.

ca. 1755
110. Untitled map of Lake George-Lake Champlain area.
> Unidentified; apparently an illustrative plate from a book. Scale not indicated. 9 x 6. Shows location of Crown Point and Fort William Henry, Ticonderoga, and Edward [N.Y.].
> Ref. Coll.

1775
111. Battle Near Lake George, September 8, 1775.
> Unidentified; apparently an illustrative plate from a book. Scale not indicated. 5½ x 9. A panel of two panoramic views of the battlefield, including a key to positions and movements of the troops.
> Ref. Coll.

1757
112. Plan of The Attack on Fort William Henry. 1757.
> Engraved by George G. Smith for George Bancroft's *History of the United States* (Boston: 1852). 1 inch to ca. 1,000 feet. 5 x 7. Key shows location of attacking troops and guns. File includes two copies. Inset: plan of the fort.
> Ref. Coll.

1758
113. Map of the Outlet of Lake Horicon to illustrate [Gen. James] Abercrombie's Attack on Ticonderoga. July 1758.
> Engraved by George G. Smith for Bancroft's *History of the United States*, cited in entry 112. Scale not indicated. 5 x 7½. Includes key to troop positions and movement.
> Ref. Coll.

1758
114. A Plan of the Town and Fort of Carillon at Ticonderoga; with the Attack made by the British Army Commanded by Genl. Abercrombie, 8 July 1758.
> Engraved by Thomas Jefferys; published 1768 by Sayer & Jefferys, London. 1 inch to 180 feet. 14 x 17. Shows topography, roads, fortifications, and troop positions.
> Ref. Coll.

1762
115. A Survey of Lake Champlain, including Lake George, Crown Point and St. John. Surveyed by Order of His Excellency Major-General Sr. Jeffery Amherst, Knight of the most Honble. Order of the Bath, Commander in Chief of His Majesty's Forces in North America. (now Lord Amherst). By William Brassier, Draughtsman, 1762.
> Published 1776 by Sayer & Bennett, London. 1 inch to ca. 6 miles. 27 x 21½. Shows topography, settlements, and the battlefields of October 1776. Inset: map of Lake George compiled in 1756 by Captain Jackson.
> RG 76: Ser. 8, No. 51.

116. Copy of map cited in entry 115. 26 x 20. Annotation: penciled grid superimposed over lake areas.
> RG 77: Ama 66.

117. An edition of map cited in entry 115. Published 1794 by Laurie & Whittle, London. 27 x 18½.
> RG 77: D72.

1766-67
118. To His Excellency Sir Henry Moore, Bart. . Captain General and Governour in Chief, In and Over His Majesty's Province of New York and the Territories depending thereon in America Chancellor and Vice Admiral of the Same. This Plan of the City of New York and its Environs, Survey's and Laid down: Is Most Humbly Dedicated by His Excellency's Most Obedt Humble Servant, B[ernard]. Ratzer Lieut. in His Majesty's 60th or Royal American Regt. [Surveyed 1766-67].
> Engraved by Thomas Kitchin; published 1776 by Jefferys & Faden, London. 1 inch to ca. 900 feet. 48 x 35½ (on 2 sheets). Shows roads, private estates, cultivated areas, numerous buildings, and a panoramic view of Manhattan Island from Governor's Island.
> RG 77: D70.

1771
119. Map of the Province of New York, 1771, Showing the Country of the Six Nations. Facsimile, published for the Eleventh Census of

INDIVIDUAL COLONIES OR STATES

1890, of a map originally titled "To His Excellency William Tryon Esqr. Captain General & Governor in Chief of the Province of New-York &c. &c. This Map of the Country of the VI Nations Proper, With Part of the Adjacent Colonies Is humbly inscribed by his Excellency's Most Obedient humble Servant Guy Johnson 1771."

> Published ca. 1890. 1 inch to ca. 40 miles. 9½ x 12. Shows locations of trails, forts, towns, and Indian tribes.

RG 29: General Records.

1772

120. Plan of Bedlow's Island Surveyed at the Request, and in the Presence, of a Committee of the Corporation of the City of New York. Containing above Highwater Mark 9 Acres and 3 Roods. Surveyed the 27th June 1772. By Gerard Banckes City Surveyor.

> Manuscript. 1 inch to 66 feet. 14½ x 19½. Annotation: "Engr. Dept. August 7, 1843. Received with Col [J. J.] Abert's letter of August 5. (A. 336)."

RG 77: Dr. 38, Sht. 1.

1776

121. A Map of the Province of New-York, Reduc'd from the large Drawing to that Province, Compiled from Actual Surveys by Order of His Execllency William Tryon, Esqr. Captain General & Governor of the Same, By Claude Joseph Sauthier; to which is added New-Jersey, from the Topographical Observations of C. J. Sauthier & B. Ratzer.

> Engraved and published 1776 by William Faden, London. 1 inch to ca. 15 miles. 31 x 24. Shows roads, counties, and towns.

RG 77: U.S. 3.

1776

122. Plan of the Country from Frogs Point to Croton River Shewing the Positions of the American & British Armies from the 12th of Oct. 1776 until the Engagement on the White Plains on the 28th.

> Engraved by J. Yeager, apparently for use as an illustrative plate in a book. 1 inch to ca. 2 miles. 10½ x 8½. Shows topography, roads, and troop positions and movements along the lower Hudson Valley above Manhattan.

Ref. Coll.

1776

123. A Plan of the Country from Frogs Point to Croton River shewing the Positions of the American and British Armies from the 12th of October 1776 until the Engagement on the White Plains on the 28th.

> Variant of map cited in entry 122 drawn by S. Lewis and "Engrav'd for Washington's Life" by B[enjamin]. Jones. Published 1807 [?] by C. P. Wayne, Philadelphia. 1 inch to 1 mile. 17 x 10½.

Ref. Coll.

1777

124. Untitled map showing Forts Clinton and Montgomery and vicinity, along the Hudson River.

> Printed by R. H. Pease, Albany, N.Y., apparently as an illustrative plate in a book. Scale not indicated. 9 x 6. Shows the two forts, topography, troop positions and movements, and naval vessels in the river.

Ref. Coll.

1776

125. Position of the American Army at New York and the Battle of Long Island, August 27th, 1776.

> Photocopy of map from an unidentified book. 1 inch to ca. 1 mile. 18½ x 11½. Shows roads, forts, and troop positions and movements on Manhattan Island and adjacent parts of Long Island.

Ref. Coll.

1776

126. Untitled map showing the Battle of White Plains.

> Printed; apparently an illustrative plate from a book. Scale not indicated. 8½ x 11. Shows topography, roads, and positions of the opposing forces.

Ref. Coll.

1776

127. Operations afer the evacuation of New York. 1776.

> Photocopy of map from an unidentified book. Scale not indicated. 16 x 10½. Shows topography, roads, forts, and troop positions in the area from upper Manhattan Island north to White Plains.

Ref. Coll.

1776

128. Fort Washington and the North Part of New York Island.
> Photocopy of map from an unidentified book. 1 inch to ca. 4,000 feet. 8 x 11½. Shows roads, fortifications, and troop positions.

Ref. Coll.

1776

129. A Topographical Map of the Northn. Part of New York Island, Exhibiting the Plan of Fort Washington, now Fort Knyphausen, shewing the several Attacks of the Royal Army.
> Engraved for Charles Stedman's *History of the American War*, published 1793. 1 inch to ca. 1,800 feet. 18½ x 11.

Ref. Coll.

1776

130. A topographic Map of the North Part of New-York Island exhibiting the Plan of Fort Washington now Fort Knyphausen, With the Rebels Lines to the Southward which where forced by the troops under the Command of The Rt. Honble. Earl Percy on the 16th Novr. 1776, and Survy'd immediately after by order of his Lordship By Claude Joseph Sauthier. To which is added the Attack made to the North by the Hessians Surveyed by Order of Lieut. Genl. Knyphausen.
> A variant at the same size and scale of map cited in entry 129. Includes red overprint showing routes of troop movements. Engraved for D. T. Valentine's *Manual* for 1859.

Ref. Coll.

1777

131. A Sketch of the Siege of Fort Schuyler [N.Y.] (1777) Presented to Col. [Peter] Gansevoort by L. Flury.
> Printed; apparently an illustrative plate from a book. Scale not indicated. 10½ x 15½. Includes key to fortifications and troop positions.

Ref. Coll.

1777

132. Plan of the Position Taken by Genl. Burgoyne on the 10th of Octr. 1777 in which the British Army was Invested by the Americans Under the Command of Genl. [Horatio] Gates and Surrendered to Him on the 16th of October the Same Year.
> Drawn by Isaac A. Chapman from an original sketch made by an American officer; engraved for the *Analectic Magazine* by G. Fairman. 1 inch to 660 feet. 10 x 16. Shows topography, roads, and troop positions and movements at the battlefield of Saratoga.

Ref. Coll.

1779

133. A Chorographical Map of the Province of New-York in North America, Divided into Counties, Manor, Patents and Townships; Exhibiting Likewise all the private Grants of Land made and located in that Province: Compiled from Actual Surveys deposited in the Patent Office at New-York, By Order of His Excellency Major General William Tryon, By Claude Joseph Sautheir, Esqr.
> Engraved and published 1779 by William Faden, London. 1 inch to ca. 5 miles. 74 x 57 (on 4 sheets). Shows topography, counties, townships, private estates, roads, and settlements.

RG 77: U.S. 7.

134. A variant of the map cited in entry 133 lacking certain overprinted colors. 81 x 58 (on 6 sheets).

RG 76: Ser. 8, No. 56.

1779

135. The Country West of Hudson's or North River Occupied by the Amerfican Army under Washington.
> From a manuscript map drawn by Lord Stirling [William Alexander]; engraved by Rae Smith for use as an illustrative plate in an unidentified book published by Virtue, Emmins, & Co., New York. 1 inch to ca. 3½ miles. 10 x 7. Shows topography, roads, and settlements along the west bank of the Hudson River between Haverstraw Bay and Newburgh.

Ref. Coll.

See also entries 1(9), 2(17, 18, 26, 27, 36-39, 42, 44, 48), and 3(6, 14, 17-21, 31a, 32a).

INDIVIDUAL COLONIES OR STATES

North Carolina

1733

136. Sketch of Cape Fear River Bar and Entrance As surveyed in 1733 by Edward Moseley.

> Manuscript tracing by Campbell (first name not indicated). 1 inch to 1½ miles. 25½ x 19½. Shows soundings. Annotation: "Engineer Dept. March 31, 1853. Received with Report of Commission on Cape Fear Entrance dated Mar. 30 1853."

RG 77: H64.

1733

137. Map of the Province of North Carolina By Edward Moseley, late Surveyor General of the said Province, 1733.

> Manuscript tracing of the original. 1 inch to ca. 5 miles. 43 x 55 (on 2 sheets). Shows streams, roads, towns, and Indian villages. Includes explanation and key to various features. Insets: maps of Brunswick or Cape Fear Harbor; Beaufort or Top Sail Inlet; and Ocacock [Ocracoke] Inlet. Also includes sailing directions for Ocracoke. Annotation: "Engineer Department, Topographical Office, September 5, 1822. Copy. [Isaac] Roberdeau, Major, T[opographical]. Engineers."

RG 77: H47.

1738

138. To His Grace Thomas Hollis Pelham Duke of Newcastle Principal Secretary of State and one of His Majesties most Honorable Privy Council, &c. This Chart of His Majesties Province of North Carolina With a full & exact description of the Sea-Coast, Latitudes, Capes remarkable Inlets, Bars, Channels, Rivers, Creeks, Shoals, depths of Water, Ebbing & Flowing of the Tides, the generally Winds Setting of the currents, Countries, Precincts, Towns, Plantations, and leading Marks, with directions for all the Navigable Inlets...

> Published. Compiled by James Wimble. 1 inch to ca. 9 miles. 24 x 38½. Shows offshore soundings and settlements along the coast. Includes sailing directions. Annotation: "Engineer Dept March 31, 1853. Rec'd with Report of Commission on Cape Fear Entrance dated March 30/53 [illegible]."

RG 77: HG2.

See also entries 1(10), 2(34), 3(24, 26), 155, 157, and 158.

Ohio

1785-87

139. Township plats of the "Old Seven Ranges."

> 79 manuscript plats of the first public lands surveyed under the Land Ordinance of 1785, compiled by a survey team under the direction of Thomas Hutchins, Geographer (later Surveyor General) of the United States. Each plat is drawn at the scale 1 inch to ½ mile and is approximately 20 x 16. Data shown includes streams, some topography, and personal names, dates, and acreage involved in the transfer of certain tracts to citizens. The plats are accompanied by eight volumes of manuscript field notes.

RG 49: Headquarters Plats.

1785-87

140. Exterior boundaries of townships in the "Old Seven Ranges."

> A partial set (23 items) of manuscript plats showing the exterior township boundaries. Each is drawn at the scale 1 inch to ½ mile; sizes vary, but most are approximately 16 x 25. Textual information includes descriptions of the boundaries and boundary markers, and data on soil quality and vegetation types.

RG 49: Exterior Boundaries.

Pennsylvania

Various dates

141. A series of 13 published facsimiles of plats of private land grants in Pennsylvania from the Revolutionary and late colonial periods. Scales are not indicated on all sheets, but each includes a written or printed description of the land or of its survey:

> (1). Lands of the London Company (5,000-acre tract in Bucks County). Surveyed by Thomas Fairman. 15½ x 9½.
>
> (2). Coxburg Tract, belonging to Gabriel Cox (315½-acre tract in Nottingham Township, Washington County).

[Two dates shown: 1780 and 1785.] 15½ x 9½.

(3). Several contiguous tracts belonging to the London Company, located in Chester County near the Newcastle County boundary, ca. 1736. 9½ x 15.

(4). Tract belonging to Henry Goldny & Co. in Bucks County along the Delaware River "20 miles above the falls." [Undated.] Surveyed by Thomas Fairman. 12 x 14½.

(5). Tract of the Pennsylvania Land Company, located in Lancaster County on Conestogoe Creek. Surveyed 1760 by John Lukens. 9½ x 15.

(6). Mt. Pleasant Tract in Washington County, belonging to Benjamin Collins. 1785. 14½ x 10.

(7). London Land Company tract on the Delaware River. [Second copy of item No. 1 in this series.]

(8). Tract in Manallin Township, Fayette County, belonging to John McCulloch. 1784. 15 x 10.

(9). Tract in Manallin Township, Fayette County, belonging to Bazil Brown. 1779. 16 x 9½.

(10). Tract on Perqueaming Creek belonging to the London Land Company. [Undated.] Surveyed by Thomas Fairman. 18 x 14½.

(11). London Land Company Tract located on an island in the Delaware River near the mouth of the Schuykill. Surveyed by Thomas Fairman. 1709. 16½ x 14.

(12). Society Tract, located on Elk River near Nottingham. 1763. 23½ x 16.

(13). Tract belonging to John Estaugh & Co., located in Chester County on Conestogoe and Mill Creeks. Surveyed 1716-17 by Isaac Taylor. 23 x 19.

1681

142. A Mapp of Ye Improved Part of Pensilvania in America, Divided Into Countyes, Townships and Lotts.

Surveyed by Thomas Holme. Annotation indicates publication date was 1681. 1 inch to ca. 3 miles. 21½ x 26. Shows townships and private estates in Bucks, Philadelphia, and Chester Counties. Inset: street plan of Philadelphia.

Ref. Coll.

1755

143. Plan of the Battle of Braddock's Defeat, At the Beginning of the Action July 9th 1755. The form of the Ground drawn on the Spot by J. C. Gilleland. 1830.

Engraved by G. W. Boynton, apparently for use as an illustrative plate in a book. 1 inch to ca. 130 feet. 9½ x 6.

Ref. Coll.

1759

144. To the Honourable Thomas Penn and Richard Penn Esqr. True and Absolute Proprietaries & Governours of the Province of Pennsylvania & Counties of Newcastle Kent & Sussex on Delaware This Map of the improved Part of the Province of Pennsylvania. Is humbly dedicated by Nicholas Scull.

Undated printed facsimile of the original. 1 inch to 4 miles. 34 x 62 (on 2 sheets). Shows generalized topography, roads, towns, forts, mines, and meeting houses in the eastern half of the colony.

Ref. Coll.

1770

145. To the Honorable Thomas Penn and Richard Penn Esquires True and Absolute Proprietaries and Governors of the Province of Pennsylvania and the Territories thereunto belonging and to the Honorable John Penn Esquire Lieutenant-Governor of the same This Map of the Province of Pennsylvania Is humbly dedicated by their Most Obedient humble Servt. W. Scull.

Published facsimile of the original engraved by Henry Dawkins and published 1770 by James Nevil. 1 inch to ca. 10 miles. 23½ x 34.

Ref. Coll.

1775

146. A Map of Pennsylvania Exhibiting not only the Improved Parts of that Province, but also its Extensive Frontiers: Laid down From Actual Surveys, and Chiefly From the late Map of W. Scull Published in 1770; And Humbly Inscribed to the Honourable Thomas Penn and Richard Penn Esquires, True and Absolute Proprietaries and Governours of the Province of Pennsylvania and the Territories thereunto belonging.

    Published 1775 by Sayer & Bennett, London. 1 inch to ca. 6 miles. 28½ x 54 (on 2 sheets). Shows topography, roads, towns, and forts.

RG 76: Ser. 30, Jefferys Atlas, No. 20.

147.   Published facsimile of the map cited in entry 146. 28½ x 49.

Ref. Coll.

1778

148. Untitled map annotated "Battle of Germantown, Pa."

    Published; apparently an illustrative plate from a book. 1 inch to ca. 1⅓ miles. 12 x 9. Shows roads in the area north of Philadelphia with key to troop positions and other features.

Ref. Coll.

1790

149. Presque Isle & Bay, at Erie, Penn., August 23d, 1790.

    Manuscript tracing of a map drawn by Andrew Ellicott. Scale not indicated. 12½ x 8.

RG 77: E113.

See also entries 2(11, 15, 16, 18, 25, 29, 31, 35-39, 44, 48), and 3(8-13).

Rhode Island

ca. 1776

150. Untitled map of Narragansett Bay.

    Manuscript. Scale not indicated. 23 x 18. Shows roads and settlements and soundings in the bay. Annotation: "Copied from De Barre's Map, 1776."

RG 77: Dr. 26, Sht. 1.

ca. 1776

151. A Plan of Rhode Island formerly Aquedneck with the Parts Adjacent Survey'd and Drawn by Chas. Blaskowitz.

    Manuscript. 1 inch to 2,000 feet. 38 x 33. Shows topography, roads, settlements, and a few soundings in the bay. Inset: Plan of Newport with a key to the principal buildings, wharves, and streets.

RG 77: C31.

1777

152. A Topographical Chart of the Bay of Narraganset in the Province of New England, with all the isles contained therein, among which Rhode Island and Connonicut have been particularly Surveyed. Shewing the true position & bearings of the Banks, Shoals, Rocks, &c. as likewise the Soundings: To which have been added the several Works & Batteries raised by the Americans. Taken by Order of the Principal Farmers on Rhode Island. By Charles Blaskowitz.

    Printed version of map cited in entry 150, varying slightly in coloring; published 1777 by William Faden, London. 1 inch to ca. ¾ mile. 38 x 26.

RG 77: U.S. 4.

1778

153. Untitled map showing positions of British and American Troops on Rhode Island in August, 1778.

    Published facsimile "Copied from the original in the possession of the Massachusetts Historical Society, 1883." 1 inch to ca. 4,000 feet. 21 x 24. Shows roads, fortifications, and troop positions and movements.

RG 77: Dr. 26, Sht. 42.

1778

154. A Map of Part of Rhode Island Showing the Positions of the American and British Armies at the Siege of Newport, and the subsequent Action on the 29th August 1778.

    Drawn by S. Lewis and engraved by Benjamin Jones for *Washington's Life* (author and publisher unknown). 1 inch to ca. 2⅓ miles. 17 x 11. Shows towns, roads, fortifications, and positions of the opposing forces.

Ref. Coll.

See also entry 1(13).

South Carolina

ca. 1685

155. A New Map of Carolina.

    A printed facsimile of the original compiled by John Thornton, Robert Morden,

and Philip Lea. 1 inch to ca. 25 miles. 20½ x 16. Shows streams and settlements along the coast of South Carolina and southern North Carolina. Includes list of names of settlements. Inset: map of the mouths of the Ashley and Cooper Rivers.
Ref. Coll.

1704

156. A Plan of Charles Town from a survey of Edw[ar]d. Crisp in 1704.

Printed map engraved by James Akin; publisher not indicated. 1 inch to 660 feet. 9 x 11½. Includes key to prominent buildings.
RG 77: Dr. 64, Sht. 4.

ca. 1775

157. A Map of North & South Carolina. Accurately copied from the old maps of James Cook, Published in 1771, and of Henry Mouzon, in 1775.

Undated published map. 1 inch to ca. 17 miles. 17½ x 22. Shows generalized topography, parishes, towns, Indian villages, and roads. Insets: plan of Beaufort, plan of Camden, plan of Charlestown [Charleston], and plan of Georgetown. Annotation: "Rec'd from Gen'l O. M. Poe with his letter of Dec 12 84."
RG 77: U.S. 409.

1775

158. An Accurate Map of North and South Carolina With Their Indian Frontiers, Shewing in a district manner all the Mountains, Rivers, Swamps, Marshes, Bays, Creeks, Harbours, Sandbanks and Soundings on the Coasts; with the Roads and Indian paths; as well as other Divisions of the Land In Both Provinces; the whole From Actual Surveys By Henry Mouzon and Others.

Published 1775 by Sayer & Bennett, London. 1 inch to ca. 9 miles. Shows counties, townships, forts, roads, and some offshore soundings. Insets: map of Port Royal Harbor and map of Charleston Harbor.
RG 76: Ser. 30, Jefferys Atlas, Nos. 23 and 24.

1776

159. An Exact Plan of Charles-Town-Bar and Harbour From an Actual Survey. With the Attack of Fort Sullivan on the 28th of June 1776. By His Majesty's Squadron. Commanded by Sir Peter Parker.

Manuscript tracing of the original published 1776 by Sayer & Bennett, London. 1 inch to ½ mile. 20 x 28. Shows towns, forts, and soundings. Key identifies locations of ships and various structures. Annotation: "Copied by Z. B. Tower Jan 21, 1842."
RG 77: Dr. 64, Sht. 5.

1779

160. Fortifications of Charleston, S.C. 1779.

Manuscript. Scale not indicated. 14 x 11½. Shows fortifications and street plan of the city. Annotation: "Presented by Robt. Mills, Architect Public Buildings, Jan 1840."
RG 77: Dr. 64, Sht. 6.

ca. 1780

161. A Sketch of the Environs of Charlestown in South Carolina.

British map published ca. 1780. 1 inch to ca. 2 miles. 17 x 23. Shows roads, settlements, fortifications, and positions of attacking British troops. Key locates and describes fortifications and troop positions.
Ref. Coll.

1780

162. A Sketch of the Operations Before Charlestown the Capital of South Carolina.

Printed facsimile of the original compiled under the command of Sir Henry Clinton and published 1780. 1 inch to ca. 1,500 feet. 26½ x 20. Shows natural vegetation, farms, roads, and fortifications in the Charleston area. Key describes and locates fortifications and British ships and encampments.
RG 77: Dr. 64, Sht. 77.
See also entries 1(14), 2(34), 3(4, 5, 5a, 7a, 24, 27, 29), and 56.

Vermont

1789

163. A Topographical Map of the State of Vermont, from actual Survey. Most humbly Dedicated To

his Excellency Thomas Chittenden Esqr. Governor and Commander in Chief; the Honorable the Council, and the Honorable the Representatives of said State; By their Most Obedient and Devoted Humble Servant William Bloget.

    Engraved and printed 1789 by Amos Doolittle, New Haven, Conn. 1 inch to ca. 4½ miles. 39 x 30½. Shows topography, roads, towns, forts, meeting houses, mills, and ironworks.

RG 77: U.S. 107.

See also entries 3(14-16).

Virginia

1606

164. Captain John Smith's Map of Virginia, 1606.
    Facsimile of the original, published by N. Peters, Washington, D.C. 1 inch to ca. 15 miles. 18½ x 22½. Shows streams and Indian villages.

RG 77: Dr. 150, Sht. 1.

1781

165. Plan of the Attacks of York[Town] in Virginia by the Allied Armies of America and France Commanded by his Excellency General Washington his Excellency the Count [de] Rochambeau Commanding the French Army.
    Manuscript. Compiled 1781 by Jean-Baptists Gouvion. 1 inch to ca. 400 feet. 37 x 28. Shows topography, roads, and fortifications around Yorktown and Gloucester. Included is a brief chronology of the siege.

RG 360.

1781

166. A Plan of the Posts of York[Town] and Gloucester in the Province of Virginia Established by His Majesty's Army under the Command of Lieut. General Earl Cornwallis together with the Attacks and Operations of the American and French Forces Commanded by General Washington and the Count of Rochambeau which Terminated in the Surrender of the Said Posts and Army on the 17th of October 1781. Surveyed by Capt. Fage of The Royal Artillery.
    Manuscript tracing of the original published 1782 in London. 1 inch to 500 feet. 27½ x 41. Shows fortifications and positions of the opposing naval vessels. Annotation: Copied from the original Feby 10th 1840. by J. G. Bruff." Inset: small-scale map of area covered by main map.

RG 75: GA 421.

See also entries 1(15), 2(2-9, 13, 18, 19, 21, 32, 33, 35, 39, 41, 45, 47, 48), and 3(24, 28, 29a, 30, 30a, 33-35).

Index

This list is indexed by entry numbers. The index consists chiefly of the names of Colonies and States, of towns and forts, rivers, lakes, and harbors, and of explorers, surveyors, mapmakers, engravers, publishers, and military and political figures who were in some way connected with the histories of specific maps. Subnumbers appearing in parentheses refer to maps in the three atlases described in part I or to the series of maps in part III under entry 141.

Abercrombie, Gen. James, 113, 114
Abert, Col. J. J., 120
Adams, John, 1(18)
Akin, James 156
Alexander, William ("Lord Stirling"), 135
Alexandria, Va., 2(19, 45)
Allegheny and Monongahela Rivers, junction of, 15
Almon, J., 48
Amboy, N. J., 49
Amelia Harbor, 73
Amherst, Maj. Gen. Jeffery, 115-117
Annapolis, Md., 2(45); harbor, 8
Aquanishuonigy, 16
Arnold, Gen. Benedict, 42, 43
Ashley River, 155

Baffin Bay, 59
Banckes, Gerard, 120
Bancroft, George, 112, 113
Barbados, 2(1)
Barres, Joseph des, 93, 95, 96, 150
Baum, Lieutenant Colonel, 3(16)
Bauman, Sebastian, 2(41)
Baxter, James P., 90, 91
Beaufort, S. C., 157
Beaufort Inlet, N. C., 137
Bedlow's Island, N. Y., 120
Belhaven. See Alexandria
Bell, Peter, 26
Bellin, Nicolas, 87
Bemis Heights, N. Y., 3(18). See also Saratoga
Bennington, Vt., 3(16)
Berkeley Springs, W. Va. 2(10)
Bew, John, 61, 80
Blainey, Jacob, 73
Blanchard, Colonel, 1(7)
Blaskowitz, Charles, 97, 98, 151, 152
Blodget, William 163

Bolton, S., 13
Bonnecamps, Reverend, 10
Boston, Mass., 2(12, 40, 42), 3(2, 2a), 94; harbor, 37, 39, 95, 96
Bouquet, Col. Henry, 28
Bowen, Emanuel, 29
Bowles, Carrington, 36
Bowles, Thomas and John, 6, 7
Boynton, G. W., 143
Braddock, Gen. Edward, 2(29, 35), 143
Braemus Heights. See Bemis Heights
Brahm, William de, 56, 83, 84
Brandywine, Pa., 2(15, 37), 3(9)
Brassier, William, 115-117
Bridges Creek. See Wakefield, Va.
Briones, Capt. Joseph, 88
Brooklyn, N. Y., 2(36)
Broom, James, 2(15)
Bruce, Normand, 2(25)
Bruff, J. G., 166
Brunswick, N.C., 137
Bryan, Hugh, 56
Bucks County, Pa. See London Land Co.; Henry Goldny & Co.
Bull, William, 56
Bunker's Hill, Mass., 3(1)
Burgoyne, Lt. Gen. John, 3(14, 17-19), 132
Burrell's Ferry, Va., 3(29)

California, Gulf of, 51; coast, 55
Cambridge, Mass., 2(12, 42)
Camden, S. C., 3(26), 157, See also Hobkirks Hill
Campbell, ____, 136
Campbell, General, 77
Campbell, Lt. Col. Archibald, 86
Canada, map of southern, 17. See also North America, map of
Cape Fear River, 136; harbor. See Brunswick, N. C.

Carillon, *See* Fort Ticonderoga
Carleton, Osgood, 95
Cartagena, Colombia, 6
Carver, Jonathan, 53, 58
Cary, John, 57
Casco Bay Fort, Maine, 90, 91
Champlain, Lake, 16, 110, 115-117
Chapman, Isaac A., 132
Charleston, S.C., 3(4, 7a, 25), 7, 156, 157, 160-162; harbor, 158, 159
Charlevoix, P. de, 87
Chesapeake & Ohio Canal. *See* Patowmack Co.
Chesapeake Bay, 3(33)
Chester, Pa., 3(11)
Chester County, Pa. *See* London Land Co.; John Estaugh & Co.
Chittenden, Thomas, 163
Churchman, John, 1(2)
Clinton, Sir Henry, 3(8, 20), 162
Cockspur Island, Ga., 84
Connecticut, 1(1), 16, 152, *See also* New England
Cook, James, 157
Cooper River, 155
Cornwallis, Maj. Gen. Charles, 3(24, 33), 166
Cowpen Creek, Fla., 77
Coxburg Tract, Pa., 141(2)
Crawford, William, 2(23)
Crisp, Edward, 156
Crown Point, N. Y., 110, 115-117
Cumberland, Md., 2(11, 12)

d'Anville, Jean Baptiste, 12, 13, 36, 45
Dawkins, Henry, 145
Delaware, 1(2, 15), 2(30), 3(24), 11, 16, 144; bay, 46
Delaware River, 3(11), 46
Dewhurst, W. W., 78, 79
District of Columbia, 2(46, 48)
Doolittle, Amos, 163
Dunn, Samuel, 58

Elizabethtown, N. J., 3(22)
Ellicott, Andrew, 149
Erie, Lake, 10, 16, 54
Erie, Pa., 149
Erskine, Robert, 2(14)
Escambia River, 72
Esnauts & Rapilly, 65
Evans, Lewis, 11, 16, 48

Faden, William, 3(1-36), 46, 56, 62, 75, 85, 86, 94, 97, 98, 105, 108, 121, 133, 134, 152. *See also* Jefferys and Faden

Fage, Captain, 166
Fairman, G., 132
Fairman, Thomas, 141(1, 4, 7, 10, 11)
Falmouth Neck, Maine, 92
Fayette County, Pa., 141(8, 9)
Ferry Farm, *See* Rappahannock Farm
Fisher, Joshua, 46
Florida, 26, 17, 29, 40, 41, 76. *See also* Amelia Harbor; Escambia River; Fort Charlotte; Fort San Marcos; Pensacola; Perdido Bay; Saint Augustine
Floyd, John, 2(23)
Flury, L., 131
Fora, Nicolas de la, 33
Forbes, Gen. John, 2(29)
Fort Carillon. *See* Fort Ticonderoga
Fort Charlotte, Fla., 68
Fort Clinton, N. Y., 3(20), 124
Fort Cumberland. *See* Cumberland, Md.
Fort Duquesne (Pittsburgh), Pa., 14. *See also* Fort Pitt
Fort Edward, 110
Fort Knyphausen. *See* Fort Washington
Fort LeBoeuf, Pa., 2(11, 29)
Fort Loudoun, Va., 2(13)
Fort Mifflin, Pa., 2(16), 3(11)
Fort Montgomery, N. Y., 3(20), 124
Fort Moultrie, S. C. *See* Fort Sullivan
Fort Pitt, 28. *See also* Fort Duguesne
Fort San Marcos, Fla., 81, 82
Fort Schuyler, N. Y., 131. *See also* Fort Stanwix
Fort Stanwix, N. Y., 34. *See also* Fort Schuyler
Fort Sullivan, S. C., 3(4-5a, 7a), 159
Fort Ticonderoga, N. Y., 110, 113, 114
Fort Washington, N. Y., 3(6), 128-130
Fort William Henry, N. Y., 110, 112
Four Mile run, Va., 2(21)
Franklin, Benjamin, 1(17)
Fraser, Brig. Gen. Simon, 3(15)
Fredericksburg, Va., 2(9, 47)
Fry, Joshua, 38

Galvez, Bernard de, 88
Gansevoort, Col. Peter, 131
Gascoigne, Capt. John, 56
Gates, Gen. Horatio, 132
George, Lake, 110, 111, 115-117
Georgetown, S. C., 157
Georgia, 1(3), 2(34), 29, 56, 86. *See also* Cockspur Island; Savannah; Savannah River
Germantown, Pa., 2(37), 3(13), 148
Gilleland, J. C., 143
Gloucester, Va., 3(33, 35), 165, 166

INDEX

Gouvion, Jean-Baptiste, 165
Grant, James, 97, 98
Grasse, Count de, 3(33)
Great Falls, Va., 2(46)
Great Kanawha River, W. Va., 2(23, 24)
Great Lakes. *See* individual names of lakes
Green, John (Bradock Mead), 37, 39
Greenland, 13
Grey, Maj. Gen. Charles, 3(10)
Griffith, Dennis, 1(4)
Guildford Courthouse, N. C., 3(26)

Halifax, Earl of, 18-25
Hancock's House, 3(31)
Hand, Gen. Edward, 2(18)
Harper's Ferry, W. Va., 2(22)
Havana, Cuba, 6
Haverstraw Bay, N. Y., 135
Haye, Guillaume de, 12
Henry Goldny & Co., 141(4)
Hills, J., 3(13)
Hills, Lieutenant, 108
Hobkirk's Hill, S. C., 3(27)
Holland, Maj. Samuel, 47, 49, 95, 97, 98
Holme, Thomas, 142
Horicon, Lake, 113
Howe, Admiral Lord Richard, 106, 107
Howe, Maj. Gen. William, 3(1, 8, 9, 12)
Hubbardton, Vt., 3(15)
Hudson Bay, 13, 18-25, 59
Hudson, highlands, 2(37)
Hudson River, 2(38, 39), 124, 135; mouth of, 49
Huron, Lake, 5
Hutchins, Thomas, 28, 54, 72, 139

Illinois country, 16
Illinois River, 54
Indian tribes, location of (Virginia to Maine), 4; nations, 16

Jackson, Captain, 115-117
James River, 3(33)
James, Thomas, 3(5a)
Jay, John, 1(6)
Jefferson, Peter, 1(15), 38
Jefferson, Thomas, 1(15), 65
Jefferys & Faden, 25, 118
Jefferys, Thomas, 17, 37, 39, 40, 41, 75, 114. *See also* Sayer & Jefferys
John Estaugh & Co., 141(13)
Johnson, Guy, 119
Johnson, Sir William, 34

Jones, Benjamin, 123, 154

Kentucky, 1(16), 2(48)
Kingsbridge, N. Y., 3(32a)
Kitchin, Thomas, 18-25, 35, 118
Knapton, John and Paul, 13
Knyphausen, Lt. Gen. Wilhelm, 3(22), 130

Labrador, 13, 18-25
Lancaster County, Pa. *See* Pennsylvania Land Co.
Langdon, Rev. John, 1(7)
Laurie & Whittle, 31, 32, 41, 117
Lawrence, William, 99
Lea, Philip, 155
Lewis, Samuel, 2(23), 123, 154
Little Kanawha River, W. Va., 2(22, 24)
Lodge, John, 61, 80
London Land Co., 141(1, 3, 7, 10, 11)
Long Island, N. Y., 125
Lotter, Matthew Albert, 50
Louis, Duke of Orleans, 13
Louisiana, 12, 17, 40, 41. *See also* New Orleans; Pontchartrain, Lake
Lukens, John, 141(5)

Macomb, Maj. Gen. Alexander, 85, 94
Maine, 1(6), 42, 43. *See also* Casco Bay Fort; Falmouth Neck; Penobscot Bay; Penobscot River
Manning, C. C., 90
Mansfield, J. K. F., 84
Maryland, 1(4, 15), 2(25, 30, 48), 3(24), 7, 16, 54. *See also* Annapolis; Cumberland
Massachusetts, 1(5, 6), *See also* Boston; Bunker's Hill; Cambridge; New England
Mead, Bradock. *See* Green, John
Merrill, Lt. Col. Wm. L., 10
Mexico, 33. *See also* Mexico City; North America, map of; Veracruz
Mexico City, Mexico, 6
Michigan, Lake, 5
Mills, Robert, 160
Mississippi River, 12-15, 65, 89; mouth of, 8
Mitchell, John, 1(6), 18-25
Mobile River, mouth of, 8
Moll, Herman, 6-9
Monmouth Courthouse, N. J., 2(38, 40), 3(36)
Montresor, Capt. John, 94
Moore, Sir Henry, 118
Morden, Robert, 155
Morristown, N. J., 2(36, 37, 44)
Moseley, Edward, 136, 137

Mount Pleasant Tract, Pa., 141(6)
Mount Vernon, Va., 2(2-7, 32)
Mouzon, Henry, 157, 158
Mowatt, ___, 92
Mulligan, J. W., 23
Muskingum River, 28

Narragangansett Bay, 1(13), 150, 152
Nevil, James, 145
Newburgh, N. Y., 2(44), 135
New Casco Fort, Maine. *See* Casco Bay Fort
New England, 2(26), 7, 9, 37, 47, 48
Newfoundland, 7, 47
New Hampshire, 1(7), 97, 98. *See also* New England
New Jersey, 1(8), 2(14, 28), 3(7, 8), 7, 9, 11, 16, 49, 50, 99, 102, 105, 121. *See also* Amboy; Elizabethtown; Monmouth Courthouse; Morristown; Princeton; Quintin's Bridge; Sandy Hook; Trenton
New Orleans, La., 87
Newport, R. I., 151, 154
New Scotland, *See* Nova Scotia
New Windsor, N. Y., 2(44)
New York, 1(9), 2(27, 48), 3(6), 7, 9, 11, 16, 43, 47, 49, 50, 118, 119, 121, 133-135. *See also* Bedlow's Island; Bemis Heights; Brooklyn; Champlain, Lake; Crown Point; Fort Clinton; Fort Montgomery; Fort Schuyler; Fort Stanwix; Fort Ticonderoga; Fort Washington; Fort William Henry; George, Lake; Haverstraw Bay; Horicon, Lake; Long Island; Newburgh; New Windsor; New York, N. Y.; Niagara River; Saratoga; Stillwater; Stony Point; Verplanck's Point; White Plains
New York, N. Y., 1(18) 2(43), 49, 125; evacuation of, 127
Niagara River, 109
Norman, William, 95
North America, map of, 8, 13, 36, 44, 45, 51, 52, 53, 59, 61; British and French dominions, 25, 26, 27, 60; British Empire, 35; Middle British Colonies, 16, 48; Spanish territories, 60
North Carolina, 1(10, 11), 2(34), 3(24), 7, 54, 137, 138, 155, 157, 158. *See also* Beaufort Inlet; Brunswick; Cape Fear River; Guildford Courthouse; Ocracoke Inlet
Nova Scotia, 7, 47

Ocracoke Inlet, N. C., 137
O'Hara, Gen. Charles, 106, 107
Ohio, 2(31, 48), 28, 48; 139, 140; Valley, 10, 34

Ohio River, 2(24)
Ontario, Lake, 10, 16
Osborne, T., 29
Osburns, Va., 3(30)

Page, Lieutenant, 3(2, 21a), 94
Parker, Commodore Peter, 3(5, 5a, 7a), 159
Patowmack Co., 2(46)
Pawpaw, W. Va., 2(21)
Pazzi, Giuseppe, 70
Pease, R. H., 124
Pelham, Thomas H., 138
Penn, John, 145
Penn, Richard, 144-147
Penn, Thomas, 144-147
Pennsylvania, 1(12, 15), 2(25, 29, 48), 3(8), 7, 9, 11, 16, 54, 141, 142, 144-147. *See also* Brandywine; Chester; Coxburg Tract; Erie; Fayette County; Fort Duquesne; Fort LeBoeuf; Fort Mifflin; Germantown: Henry Goldny & Co.; John Estaugh & Co.; London Land Co.; Pennsylvania Land Co.; Philadelphia; Society Tract; Trudruffin; Valley Forge; White Horse Tavern
Pennsylvania Land Co., 141(5)
Penobscot Bay, 93
Penobscot River, 93
Pensacola, Fla., 68, 76, 77
Percy, Sir Hugh, 3(6), 130
Perdido Bay, Fla., 77
Peters, N., 164
Petersburg, Va., 3(28)
Philadelphia, Pa., 2(16, 44), 3(11, 12), 142
Phillips, Major General, 3(28)
Pine Grove. *See* Rappahannock Farm, Va.
Poe, Gen. O. M., 157
Pontchartrain, Lake, 88
Pope's Creek, 2(8)
Porter, Peter A., 109
Porto Bello, Panama, 6
Port royal, S. C., 158
"Post Route Map," 9
Potomac River, 2(8, 22, 32)
Pownall, Thomas, 47-49, 51, 52, 59
Prevost, Maj. Gen. Augustin, 3(23), 85
Princeton, N. J., 2(36), 101, 103, 104
Purcell, Joseph, 72, 74, 76, 77-79

Quebec, Canada, 3(3), 35; Province, 47, 49, 50
Quintin's Bridge, N. J., 3(32)

Rahl, Colonel, 101

Rappahannock Farm, Va., 2(9)
Ratzer, Bernard, 118, 121
Redknap, J., 90, 91
Rhode Island, 1(13), 150-154. *See also* Narragansett Bay; New England; Newport
Richardson, William, 35
Richmond, Va., 3(29a)
Riedesel, Maj. Gen. F. von, 3(15)
Roberdeau, Maj. Isaac, 137
Robert Clarke & Co., 28
Rochambeau, Count de, 165, 166
Romans, Bernard, 1(1, 3)
Ross, Lieutenant, 30-32
Russell, Capt. W. T., 81

Saint Augustine, Fla., 6, 66, 67, 69-71, 74-76, 78-81
Saint Johns, N. Y., 115-117
Saint Lawrence Valley, 10
Sandy Hook Bar, N. J., 106-108
Saratoga, N. Y., 3(19), 132
Sasquesehanock, 8
Sauthier, Claude Joseph, 50, 121, 130, 133, 134
Savannah, Ga., 3(23), 85
Savannah River 83, 86
Sayer & Bennett, 44, 45, 47, 49, 51, 52, 58, 60, 115, 116, 146, 147, 158, 159
Sayer & Jefferys, 38, 114
Sayer, Robert, 30, 40
Scull, Nicholas, 144
Scull, William, 145-147
Seale, R. W., 13, 36
Shallus, Francis, 42
Smith, Alexander, 32
Smith, Capt. John, 164
Smith, George G., 112, 113
Smith, Rae, 135
Society Tract, Pa., 141(12)
South Carolina, 1(14), 2(34), 3(24), 7, 29, 56, 155, 157, 158. *See also* Burrell's Ferry; Camden; Charleston; Fort Sullivan; Hobkirk's Hill
Spencer's Ordinary, Va., 3(30a)
Sproule, George, 97, 98
Stedman, Charles, 129
Steuben, Major General von, 3(28)
Stevens, B. F., 22
Stillwater, N. Y., 3(17, 18). *See also* Bemis Heights and Saratoga
Stirling, Lord. *See* Alexander, William
Stony Point, N. Y., 2(17), 3(21)
Stuart, John, 56, 76
Sullivan's Island. *See* Fort Sullivan
Superior, Lake, 5

Susquehanna River, 2(18)

Tanner, H. S., 100
Taylor, Isaac, 141(13)
Tennessee, 1(11)
Thornton, John, 155
Ticonderoga. *See* Fort Ticonderoga
Tour, Brion de la, 65
Tower, Z. B., 159
Trenton, N. J., 2(36), 100, 101, 103
Trudruffin, Pa., 3(10)
Trumbull, John, 2(40)
Tryon, Maj. Gen. William, 119, 121, 133, 134
Turner, James, 48

United States of America, 1(17, 19), 2(50), 57, 58, 60, 62, 65; northeastern and north central regions, 17; southwestern, 33
Urrutia, Jose, 33

Valentine, D. T., 130
Valley Forge, Pa., 2(37, 38)
Vaughan, Samuel, 2(7)
Veracruz, Mexico, 6
Vermont, 163. *See also* Bennington; Hubbardton; Walmscock
Verplanck's Point, N. Y., 2(17)
Virginia, 1(15, 16), 2(33, 48), 3(24), 7, 16, 38, 54, 164. *See also* Alexandria; Four Mile Run; Fredericksburg; Gloucester; Great Falls; Mount Vernon; Osburns; Petersburg, Rappahannock Farm; Richmond; Spencer's Ordinary; Wakefield; Williamsburg; Winchester; Yorktown
Virtue, Emmins, & Co., 135

Wakefield, Va., 2(8)
Wallis, John, 63
Walmscock, Vt., 3(16)
Washington, George, 1(18), 2(1-50), 3(7), 3(13), 3(33), 15, 101, 165, 166
Washington, Lawrence, 2(3)
Wayne, Brig. Gen. Anthony, 3(21)
Wayne, C. P., 42, 123
West Indies, 6, 35, 44, 51, 59
Westmoreland County, Va., 2(8)
West Virginia, 1(15), 2(25, 31, 48). *See also* Berkeley Springs; Great Kanawha River; Harper's Ferry; Little Kanawha River; Pawpaw
Wheeler, Thomas, 97, 98
White Horse Tavern, Pa., 3(10)
White Plains, N.Y., 2(36), 122, 123, 126, 127

White River, mouth of, 31
Wilkinson, James, 101, 104
Williamsburg, Va., 2(47)
Wimble, James, 138
Winchester, Va., 2(13)
World, map of, showing George Washington memorials, 2(49)

Wright, H. G., 73
Wright, Thomas, 97, 98

Yeager, J., 43, 122
York River, 3(33)
Yorktown, Va., 2(39, 41), 3(33-35), 165
Yules, D. L., 73